# *It Is Easy* BEING GREEN!

## 60 Bible Stories & Crafts

With the Earth in Mind

**Abingdon Press**

Nashville

*Abingdon's*
*It Is Easy Being Green:*
*60 Bible Stories & Crafts*
*With the Earth in Mind, Ages 6–9*

Requests for permission should be addressed in writing to:
Abingdon Press, 201 Eighth, Avenue, South, Nashville, TN 37202;
or submitted by e-mail to *permissions@abingdonpress.com.*

Scripture quotations noted CEB are from the Common English Bible.
Copyright © 2011 by the Common English Bible. All rights reserved.
Used by permission. *(www.CommonEnglishBible.com)*

Scripture quotations marked (CEV) are from the Contemporary English Version
Copyright © 1991, 1992, 1995 by American Bible Society, Used by Permission.

Scripture quotations marked (NRSV) are from the New Revised Standard Version
of the Bible, copyright 1989, Division of Christian Education of the National
Council of the Churches of Christ in the United States of America.
Used by permission. All rights reserved.

Written and edited by: LeeDell Stickler
Production Editors: Charlotte Overlay and Theresa P. Kuhr
Art Credits: Brenda Gilliam, Megan Jeffery, Barbara Ball
Photo Credits: Shutterstock, Mark Foltz, Ron Benedict
Cover and Design: Florence Davis

PACP00857747-01

ISBN-13: 978-1-4267-1605-8

11 12 13 14 15 16 17 18 19 20—10 9 8 7 6 5 4 3 2 1

Printed in the U. S. A.

**FSC**
Mixed Sources
Product group from well-managed
forests, controlled sources and
recycled wood or fiber

Cert no. SCS-COC-002464
www.fsc.org
©1996 Forest Stewardship Council

# TABLE OF CONTENTS

## OLD TESTAMENT STORIES

# New Testament Stories

# HOW TO USE THIS RESOURCE

Sometimes all you need is a Bible story that will engage the children and a craft project to reinforce it. Now you can also make the craft project eco-friendly. These session guides give you clever ways to reuse, recycle, and re-purpose items that are normally thrown in the trash, as you teach an important Bible message.

**It Is Easy Being Green** walks you through the Bible with 60 interactive Bible stories.

Each story is matched with a Bible verse to learn, an earth-friendly craft activity to do, and a Green Message to reinforce.

The craft activities in this book use "recycled" items that are common to most households. All you have to do is send out a list of what you need, and soon you will have more bottle caps, milk cartons, cardboard tubes, and plastic containers than you can possibly use (or store).

Each session guide is short and to the point. The patterns, diagrams, and photographs in the cut-away reproducibles will make using this resource easier than you think.

At the back of the book is a Scripture index for your convenience. You can supplement other curriculum by matching the Scriptures and/or stories. Have fun!

## Basic Supplies

- scissors
- glue sticks
- chenille stems
- craft glue
- masking tape
- duct tape
- clear tape

- string or yarn
- crayons or markers
- paper punch
- stapler, staples
- drinking straws
- construction paper
- copy paper

- art tissue
- pencils
- colored electrical tape
- battery-operated tea lights
- wooden beads
- paper fasteners

## Recyclables

- cardboard tubes
    paper towel, wrapping paper, aluminum foil, plastic wrap
- plastic containers
    margarine tubs, yogurt cups, pudding cups
- plastic lids
- paper cartons
    8-oz. milk or juice
- fabric scraps
- small gift boxes with lids
- scrap paper

- scrap cardboard
- scrap cardstock
    or used file folders
- plastic bottles
    water, 1-quart milk, 2-liter soda
- plastic bottle caps
- plastic jars
    (such as peanut butter)
- metal cans
    soup (10 ¾ and 15 oz)
    tuna or cat food
- magazines
- newspapers

- food boxes
    cookie, cracker, cake, cereal, snack, rice, etc.
- envelopes
    business-sized, 9- by 12-inch shipping
- CDs, CD jewel cases
- paper bags
    lunch-sized, grocery
- gift wrapping paper
- refrigerator magnet
    advertisements or calendars

# How It All Began

**Bible Story**
Genesis 1:1–2:4

**Bible Verse**
God saw everything he had made: it was supremely good.
   Genesis 1:31, CEB

**Green Message**
God created the earth and all that is in it.

In the beginning there was a lot of space, a few rocks here and there, and globs of water—all with no particular place to go. God looked around at all the stuff and said, "Something should be done with all this stuff." So God whispered in the darkness and said, "Let there be light." In the time it took to speak the words, light appeared. *"Hmm,"* said God. "This is good, but it's not finished yet."

God put a great dome in the middle of the waters. There was water above the dome and water below the dome. "This is good," said God, "but it's not finished yet."

So God put all the waters below the dome in one place. When this happened, dry land appeared. "This is good," said God, "but it's not finished yet."

God caused the dry land to grow plants of every kind, plants that could make seeds so that there would be more plants. There were big plants and little plants. There were plants with flowers and plants with fruits. "This is good," said God, "but I'm not finished yet."

God filled the sky with lights. These lights shone down on the earth. There were lights for the daytime and lights for the night. There were plants growing everywhere. "This is good," said God, "but it's not finished yet."

God put fish in the water and birds in the air. God put animals of every kind on the earth. "This is good," God said, "but I'm not finished yet. I need someone to take care of all that I have created."

So God created a man and a woman and told them, "This is my creation. You are in charge of it all."

God looked around at everything. Everything had a place. "This is not just good," said God. "This is *supremely* good." And then God rested.

## Supplies ••••••••••••••••••••••••••••••••••••••••

| | | |
|---|---|---|
| **clear 2-liter bottles** | **potting soil** | **mallet to crush charcoal** |
| **utility knife** | **sand** | **small plants, moss, rocks** |
| **masking tape** | **large containers, scoops** | **decorative items** |
| **permanent marker** | **charcoal briquettes** | **wooden craft sticks** |
| **small pebbles** | **plastic sandwich bags** | **spray bottle with water** |

## *Ahead of time:*

- Place soil, sand, and pebbles in large containers with scoops.
- Prepare the soda bottles.
  - a. Remove the labels.
  - b. Draw a line around each bottle about eight inches up.
  - c. Cut along the line with a utility knife.
  - d. Cover the cut edges with tape.

## *Group time:*

- Read "How It All Began."
- Take a Creation walk (weather permitting). Observe the world around your church building. Even in a urban setting there are living things in abundance. Let the children collect rocks, sticks, and other decorative items for their terrarium.

HINT: *Use the technique pictured on page 35 to make a level cutting line on the bottle. Stack books to raise a permanent marker to where the cut should be. Tape the marker in place, and then turn the bottle.*

- Have each child make a terrarium to have a better understanding of the interdependency of all things in God's Creation.

## CREATION TERRARIUM

1. Place a layer of pebbles in the bottom half of the bottle, about one inch deep.

2. Add a layer of sand, about one half inch deep, on top of the pebbles.

3. Put two or three charcoal briquettes in a plastic bag. Pound until the charcoal is mostly small pieces. *(Do not use match-light charcoal.)* Add this on top of the sand.

4. Add a layer of potting soil, about two inches deep.

5. Add small plants, rocks, moss, and other decorative items. Use a wooden craft stick to make planting easier.

6. Mist the terrarium until the soil is moist but not wet.

7. To close the top of the terrarium, first place the top inside the bottom at an angle as shown. Then pull the top up until the taped edges meet.

HINT: *If the container becomes foggy, open the cap and let the excess moisture evaporate.*

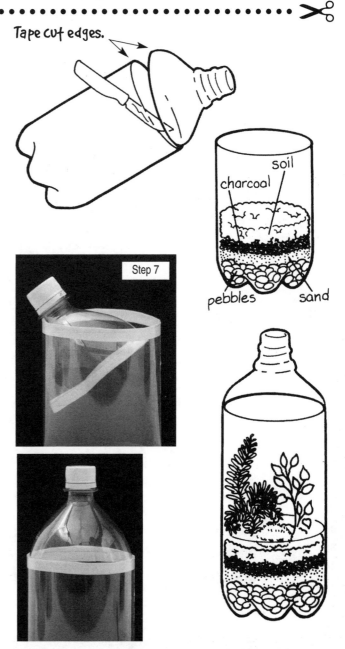

Tape cut edges.

soil
charcoal
pebbles   sand

Step 7

7

# In God's Image

**Bible Story**
Genesis 1:27-31

**Bible Verse**
God created humanity in God's own image.
Genesis 1:27, CEB

**Green Message**
God created us to reflect God's image in the world.

On the day that God created human beings, God had thought long and hard. There were fish in all the waters. There were birds in the air. There were all kinds of living creatures on the land doing just what living creatures are supposed to do.

"But there are no living things who can enjoy all that I have put on the earth," God said. "There are no creatures who can stop and enjoy a sunset or a new snowfall. There are no creatures who can marvel at an icicle or a new flower. There are no living things who can think or dream or plan for the future. There are no living things who can imagine or create. There are no living things who know the difference between right and wrong."

So on the sixth day of Creation, God made human beings, male and female. God did not make them like the fish or the birds. God did not make them like the animals who walked on the earth. God made them in God's own image, and God blessed them.

God made human beings who came in different sizes and shapes. God made human beings who came in different colors. God made human beings who had different likes and dislikes. God made human beings who could do different things.

God made artists and musicians. God made planners and builders. God made writers and readers. God made preachers and teachers. God made runners and walkers. God made baseball players and computer operators. God made cake bakers and farmers. And God made YOU (*point to one of the children*) and YOU (*point to another child*) and YOU and YOU and YOU! (*Continue pointing until you have pointed at each of the children.*)

God filled the world with people—all made in the image of God.

And that is why, boys and girls, on the very last day of Creation, God was very pleased. There were people who could enjoy and marvel and wonder and create and dream and imagine and praise God for everything. Amen.

## *Supplies* •••••••••••••••••••••••••••••••••••••••••

| | | |
|---|---|---|
| **old CD jewel cases** | **tape** | **scrapbook paper or** |
| **small craft mirrors** | **scissors** | **colored paper** |
| **craft glue or glue gun** | **pencils** | **photographs** |

## *Ahead of time:*

- Take close-up photographs of each of the children in the group. Print them out prior to the session.
- Trace the oval pattern below onto lightweight cardboard to use as a pattern.

## *Group time:*

- Talk about the days of Creation and what God created on each day.
  - Day 1—day and night
  - Day 2—the sky
  - Day 3—the earth and the sea
  - Day 4—plants
  - Day 5—fish and birds
  - Day 6—animals and human beings
- Ask: Why do you think God created human beings last?
- Pass around a mirror and let the children take turns looking at themselves.

- Explain that what they are looking at is called an "image."
- Read "In God's Image."
- Remind the children that while they are NOT God, they can **reflect** God in what they say and do.
- Talk about what these qualities might be.
- Make the "Reflecting God's Image" picture frame and mirror as a reminder to reflect God's image in the world.

### "REFLECTING GOD'S IMAGE" FRAME

1. Open the jewel case and remove the paper insert and the molded plastic piece into which the CD fits.
2. Trace the paper insert onto colored paper to make a rectangle that will fit inside the jewel case. Cut out the rectangle.
3. Trace the oval pattern onto the center of the rectangle. Cut the oval out.
4. Tape the photograph to the back side of the paper rectangle, centered on the opening.
5. Slip the sheet of paper and photograph into the jewel case as shown here.
6. Decorate the outside of the frame with small craft mirrors.

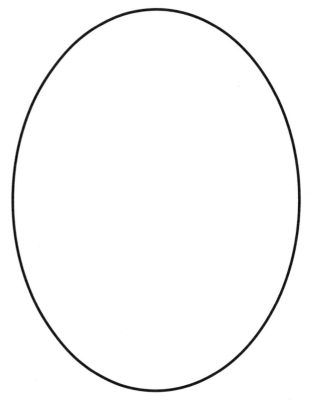

# The New Caretakers

**Bible Story**
Psalm 8

**Bible Verse**
You let us rule
everything your
hands have made.
    Psalm 8:6, CEV

**Green Message**
We should treat God's
creation with respect.

In the very beginning, there was God. From out of the rocks, and water, and a whole bunch of emptiness, God created a world. It was a beautiful world, filled with beautiful things. Then God created human beings—male and female. God blessed them. Then God gave them a job.

"Look around you, I made everything that you see," God said, "and everything that you see now belongs to you. Take care of it for me. Have children. Live in every place that can be lived in. But remember, you are in charge. You are in charge of the Sky, the Sea, and the Earth. You are in charge of the plants, the fish, the birds and the animals. You will take care of what I have created."

The human beings were worried. "How can we be in charge of such a big place? We are small and weak. We are not powerful like you are. There is so much to take care of. What happens if we make a mistake?" they asked.

"We will work together," God promised. "If you make mistakes, and you will, then I will help you fix them. I will always be there for you. There is nothing we cannot do if you pay attention and we work together."

So God placed human beings in charge of God's most wonderful creation. Most of the time human beings are mindful of their job. When they take good care of God's creation, everything goes smoothly.

But sometimes human beings get *so* busy doing other things, that they forget the job God gave them. They make mistakes. They are careless. They do not take good care of God's creation. That is when they remember what God told them, "There is nothing we can't do when we do it together."

## Supplies ..................................................

| | | |
|---|---|---|
| duct tape | pencils | empty cereal boxes |
| paper clips | scissors | |
| decorative items | craft glue | |

## Ahead of time:

- Photocopy the directions and diagram for each child.
- Disassemble the cereal boxes so that they are ready to work on.

## Group time:

- Ask: Why is it important to care for God's Creation? What will happen if we don't respect what God has created?
- Point out that when we treat God's Creation with respect, then people say we are "walking gently on the earth."

- Read "The New Caretakers."
- Ask: What does God promise us as we take on our role as "caretakers?"
- Create the Walk Gently Sandals.

### "WALK GENTLY" SANDALS

1. Open a cereal box out flat. (One cereal box will make a single pair of sandals.)
2. Trace around both of your shoes on the cereal box. (Ask a friend to help.)
3. Cut out two of each shoe (two right shoes, two left shoes).
4. Cut the extra cardboard into 1 ½-inch strips. These will be the straps. Make as many straps as you want.
5. With the help of a friend, fit the straps over the foot and around to the back of each of the cardboard shoes. Tape with duct tape.
6. Glue the second shoe print to the first, sandwiching the ends of the straps between the two. Clip with paper clips until the glue dries.
7. Decorate with a variety of items: pompoms, silk flowers, silly faces, and so forth. (See some examples below.)

HINT: *These sandals should be worn indoors as they may be slippery on certain surfaces.*

# Noah and the Flood

**Bible Story**
Genesis 6–9

**Bible Verse**
As long as the earth exists, seedtime and harvest, cold and hot, summer and autumn, day and night will not cease.
Genesis 8:22, CEB

**Green Message**
We can always depend on God's promises.

In the beginning, God created a wonderful world, filled with plants, birds, fish and animals of every sort. People of every sort lived in God's world. Everything was good. The people remembered God and thanked God for all the wonderful things God had given them. But after awhile, the people forgot about God. Only one man and his family remained faithful. His name was Noah.

One day God said to Noah, "Noah, I am not happy with the way things are on the earth. All the people mistreat one another and are wicked—all except for you and your family. I want to start all over again. I am going to send a great flood. I want you to build a boat—a very big boat."

So Noah, in a land far from the nearest sea, built a boat— a very big boat. God said to him, "Now, fill the boat with animals, two of every kind on the earth." Noah gathered the animals to go in his boat, two of every kind just as God had told him. There were so many animals that Noah lost count.

When the animals were inside, it began to rain. It rained and rained and rained. Then it rained some more. Soon water covered everything, even the tallest mountain. But Noah and his family and the animals were safe and dry.

After many days, God sent a wind to dry up the waters. Slowly the waters fell and dry land began to appear. One day Noah sent out a dove. When the dove returned, it was carrying a leafy twig. Noah knew that the earth was almost ready. When Noah sent out the dove a second time, the dove did not return. Noah knew that it was time to leave the boat.

Two by two the animals left the boat. Then Noah made a special offering to God, giving thanks for keeping them safe. Suddenly, up in the sky, a rainbow stretched from horizon to horizon. "This is a sign of my promise to you and all the earth," said God. "I will never again send a flood to destroy my creation." And to this day, God has kept that promise.

## Supplies ...............................................

| | | |
|---|---|---|
| paper towel tubes | recycled magazines | colored copy paper |
| aluminum foil | glue sticks | scissors |
| sunflower seeds | tape | mop or broom handle |

## Ahead of time:
- Tear aluminum foil into 30-inch sheets.
- Photocopy the rainstick end caps on colored copy paper.
- Tear colorful pages from recycled magazines.

## Group time:
- Make the rainsticks.
- Read "Noah and the Flood." When the time comes for the rain to fall, let the children turn their rainsticks over and over.
- Ask: How does God's special promise make you feel?
- Remind the children that God's promises are reliable.

---

### RAINSTICK

1. Fold a sheet of aluminum foil over and over until it is about ½ inch wide. Then coil it around a broomstick or mop handle to make a spiral. (See photo.)
2. Cut out the Bible verse circles. Cut flaps around each circle, stopping at the inside circle as shown.
3. Place one end cap over the end of a paper towel tube. Tape the flaps down as shown.
4. Insert the aluminum foil spiral into the tube. Then add a half cup of sunflower seeds.
5. Add the second end cap, sealing the tube.
6. Cut colorful magazine pages into 6-inch strips of various widths.
7. Glue the strips around the tube, overlapping as you work your way down.

As long as
the earth exists,
seedtime and harvest,
cold and hot,
summer and autumn,
day and night
will not cease.
Genesis 8:22, CEB

As long as
the earth exists,
seedtime and harvest,
cold and hot,
summer and autumn,
day and night
will not cease.
Genesis 8:22, CEB

# A Time for Everything

## Bible Story
Ecclesiastes 3:1-8

## Bible Verse
God makes everything happen at the right time.
Ecclesiastes 3:11, CEV

## Green Message
In God's creation, there is a plan for everything.

**Refrain: Everything on earth has a time and a season. God makes everything happen at the right time.**

There is a time to be born....
And a time to grow up.
There is a time to learn....
And a time to use what we have learned.
There is a time to try...
And a time to fail...
And a time to try again. **(Refrain)**

There is a time for spring and summer...
And a time for fall and winter.
There is a time to plant seeds...
And a time to harvest that which we have planted.
There is a time to work very hard...
And a time to rest from our work. **(Refrain)**

There is a time to dance and sing...
And a time to sleep.
There is a time to be with friends...
And a time to be by yourself.
There is a time to have angry feelings...
And a time to feel love. **(Refrain)**

There is a time to be happy....
And a time to be sad.
There is a time to fight....
And a time to make up.
There is a time to speak out...
And a time to keep quiet. **(Refrain)**

There is a time to live...
And a time to die. **(Refrain)**

God has made everything suitable for its time.
That is God's gift to us. Thank you, God.

## Supplies

| | | |
|---|---|---|
| **metal cans** (cat food, tuna fish) | **black construction paper** | **scissors** |
| **towels** | **toothpick or push pin** | **clear tape** |
| | **glue sticks** | **battery-operated tea lights** |

## Ahead of time:

• Photocopy the seasonal designs. Cut the designs apart, leaving some white space around each one.

## Group time:

• Talk with the boys and girls about the different seasons and the kinds of activities they do during each season.
• Ask: Are there things that you can do now that you couldn't do last year? two years ago? when you were a baby?

• Read "A Time for Everything." The children will say the refrain together.
• Create the "Celebrate the Seasons" night-light.

✂

### "CELEBRATE THE SEASONS" NIGHT-LIGHT

1. Fold a two-inch cuff along one of the long edges of the construction paper.
2. Cut flaps along the edge up to the fold line as shown below.
3. Place the paper on a folded towel.
4. Place each seasonal design on the paper. Tape lightly to hold in place.
5. Go around the edges with a toothpick.
6. Wrap the paper around the can, taping the flaps to the bottom as shown. Trim if necessary to fit the can.

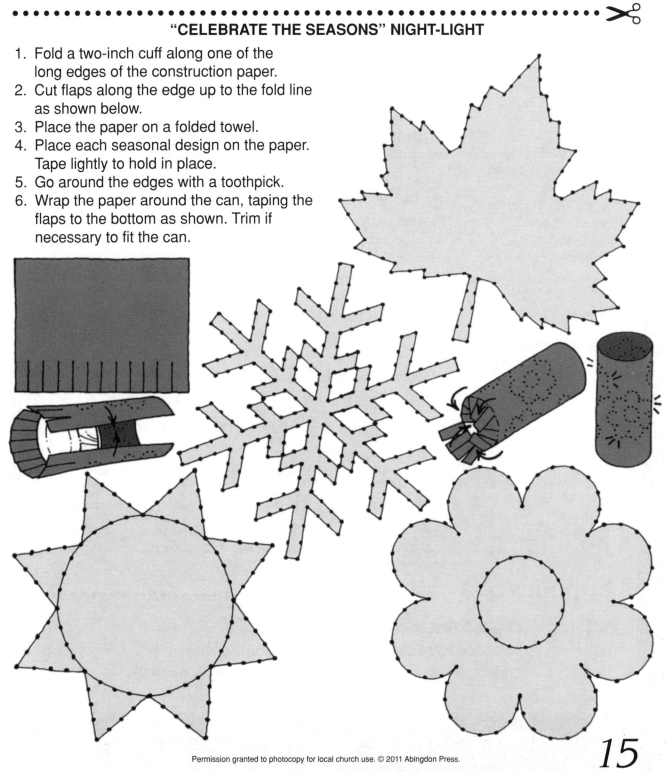

# Sharing the Land

**Bible Story**
Genesis 12:1-3;
  13:1-12

**Bible Verse**
Tell them to do good, to be rich in the good things they do, to be generous, and to share with others.
  1 Timothy 6:18, CEB

**Green Message**
When God's people share with one another, there is enough for everyone.

God said to Abraham, "Leave your country. Go to the land that I will show you. If you do this, I will make you great a blessing to all the nations." Abraham wanted to be a blessing so he and his wife Sarah and their nephew Lot set off as God told them. When they came to the land of Canaan, God said, "This is the land I promised to you. It will belong to you forever."

God blessed Abraham and his family just as God had promised. They had so many sheep and goats that they could not count them. They were rich beyond measure. Life was good.

But one day an argument broke out between the shepherds who took care of each family's sheep. "Move your flocks," said the shepherds who cared for Abraham's flocks. "There is not enough grass and water for both of our flocks."

"We won't move," said the shepherds who cared for Lot's flocks. "YOU should go somewhere else."

"This arguing has to stop," said Abraham. "Families should live together peacefully. Families should share," Abraham said to his nephew. "Our flocks have grown so large that there is not enough grass and water for both of them. We will divide the land."

*"Abraham is the head of the family. He will probably choose the best land,"* thought Lot to himself. *"It is only right."* But instead, Abraham let Lot go first.

"What if I choose to go to the north?" asked Lot.

"Then I will go to the south," said Abraham.

"What if I choose to go to the south?" asked Lot.

"Then I will go to the north," said Abraham. "We will not disagree. We will share the land. We will live in peace."

The two families separated and went in different directions.

Then God said to Abraham, "Look all around you. This land where your flocks are grazing will belong to you and to your descendants forever."

## Supplies ••••••••••••••••••••••••••••••••••••••••••

| | |
|---|---|
| 18 plastic bottle caps | scissors |
| 15-ounce soup cans | colored paper |
| craft glue | spray paint (optional) |

## Ahead of time:

- Photocopy "The Sharing Game." Optional: spray paint the soup cans.

## Group time:

- Draw a circle on the floor that is only big enough for one child. Then have all the children try to fit inside of it.
- Ask: How did it feel to be all crowded together?
- Read "Sharing the Land."
- Talk with the children about why it was not only good to share, it was necessary for the well-being of the animals.
- Make the "Sharing Game."

• • • • • • • • • • • • • • • • • • • • • • • • • • • • • • • • • • • • • • • • • • • • • • • • • ✂

### THE SHARING GAME

1. Wrap the can with colored paper.
2. Glue the Bible verse to the front of the can and the game rules to the back of the can.
3. Cut out the letters. Glue one letter onto each bottle cap. Put the caps in the can.

SUPER COOL OPTION: *Spray paint the cans before the session begins. Use bright primary colors.*

---

**How to Play the Sharing Game**
**(2 players)**

- Put the letter caps in the can and shake.
- Spill the caps out onto the table.
- Using only letters you can see, try to spell SHARE. (Question marks may be used to stand for whichever letter you wish.)
- Put the letters you are not using back in the can and try again.
- The first one to spell SHARE and say the Bible verse wins the game.

---

**Tell them to do good, to be rich in the good things they do, to be generous, and to share with others.**

1 Timothy 6:18, CEB

---

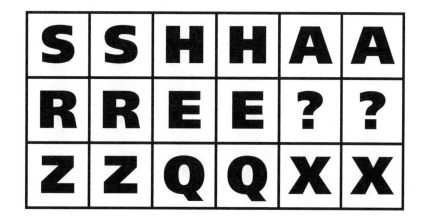

# Two Brothers

## Bible Story
Genesis 25:19-24;
27:1-45

## Bible Verse
Doing what is right
and fair pleases the
LORD.
  Proverbs 21:3 CEV

## Green Message
God wants us to do
what is right and to
treat all people fairly.

Isaac was the son of Abraham and Sarah. When he grew up, he married Rebekah. They had twin boys named Esau and Jacob. Even though they were twins, no two boys could have been more different. Esau loved to hunt and bring home meat to eat. Jacob liked to stay around the tents and help his mother. The older they became, the more different they became.

Isaac was getting old and knew it was time to give his oldest son the special blessing of God. Esau had been born first, so he would get the blessing. Jacob thought that this was unfair.

Isaac called Esau into his tent, "Esau, I am old and will soon die. Before I die, I want to give you your blessing. Go get some meat and make that special dish I love. Then I will give you God's blessing for the first son."

Rebekah overheard what Isaac was about to do. She loved her son Esau, but she loved Jacob even more. "Jacob," said Rebekah, "we are going to trick your father into giving you the blessing of the first son before Esau gets back."

"But Esau and I are very different. Esau is hairy; my skin is smooth. Father will know the difference when he touches me?" said Jacob. But Rebekah smiled. She had a plan.

Rebekah wrapped Jacob's arms in goat skin. Then she prepared a special meal for Isaac. Jacob took the food to his father and asked for his blessing. Isaac reached out to touch his son. He could feel Esau's hairy arms. So Isaac gave Jacob the blessing. Now Jacob would have a prosperous life.

When Esau came in from hunting, he prepared the food his father had asked for and took it to him. "Here I am, father. Bless me," said Esau kneeling at his father's feet.

"You are too late, my son," said Isaac. "I have already given the blessing to your brother." Esau was so angry. He wanted to kill his brother. Rebekah sent Jacob away from the tents before Esau could catch him.

## Supplies ••••••••••••••••••••••••••••••••••••••••••

**old file folders**          **glue sticks**
**scissors**                   **variety of textures**

## *Ahead of time:*

• Cut scrap cardboard into 2 ½- by 4-inch cards. (An old file folder will make about 16 cards.) Each child will want to make one set of cards.

## *Group time:*

• Prepare one set of the texture cards. Pass them around the circle and let the children feel the different textures. Then have them close their eyes and repeat the process. Have them explain the difference.
• Ask: What do you think it would be like to be blind? How would you know about your world? Would that be easy or hard?

• Read the story "Two Brothers."
• Ask: How was Jacob able to trick his father so easily? Do you think it was fair? Do you think the special blessing was fair? What could Jacob have done instead of tricking his father?
• Have the children each make a set of the texture cards.

• • • • • • • • • • • • • • • • • • • • • • • • • • • • • • • • • • • • • • • • • ✂

### TEXTURE MATCHING CARDS

1. Cut two samples (about 1 ½ inches by 2 ½ inches, but the shape can be irregular) from each kind of texture.
2. Glue each sample onto one of the cards. For example, two cards will have sandpaper, two cards will have newspaper, two cards will have fabric.
3. Place the cards face up on the table.

4. Close your eyes and try to match the cards with the same texture on them.
5. Invite a friend to play the game.

SOME SUGGESTED TEXTURES: *silk, faux fur, sandpaper, plastic canvas, leather, wool, flannel, upholstery material, wax paper, aluminum foil, notebook paper, plastic theme sleeve covers, magazine paper.*

# Joseph's Bad Day

**Bible Story**
Genesis 37

**Bible Verse**
Love is kind and patient, never jealous, boastful, proud, or rude.
   1 Corinthians 13:4, CEV

**Green Message**
God wants us to treat one another with kindness and love.

Jacob had twelve sons. Jacob loved all of his sons, but he loved his son Joseph most of all. One day Jacob gave Joseph a beautiful coat, a coat that was much nicer than any coat his other brothers owned. Joseph's brothers were very jealous.

One morning Joseph found his brothers. He was very excited. "Last night I dreamed that all of you were wheat and you bowed down to me. Then I dreamed that all of you were stars and you bowed down to me." This made Joseph's brothers dislike him even more.

One day the brothers were far away from home, keeping watch over their family's flocks. Jacob sent Joseph out to check on them. When the brothers saw Joseph coming, they said, "Here comes that little tattletale. He'll go back and tell Father that we are up to no good," they said.

"I've got an idea," said Simeon, "Let's kill him!"

"You can't kill him! He's your brother," said Reuben. "Let's throw him into that old dry well over there. That will teach him a lesson." Everyone agree to do that.

When Joseph came to the campsite, his brothers jumped him, took his new coat, and threw him into a dry well. Reuben went to check on the sheep. He planned to come back later and rescue Joseph from the well.

"Look," said one brother, "a caravan of traders going to Egypt. Let's sell Joseph to those traders as a slave." And so they did.

When Reuben returned to the camp, he looked in the well. "What have you done with him?" he asked. The brothers told him how they had sold Joseph to some traders. "What are we going to tell Father?" asked Reuben.

The brothers had not thought about that. So they killed a goat from their herd and rolled Joseph's beautiful coat in the goat's blood. "We'll tell Father that a wild animal got him." That was the plan and that is what they did.

## Supplies ●●●●●●●●●●●●●●●●●●●●●●●●●●●●●●●●●●

**recycled envelopes**
**glue sticks**
**crayons or markers**

**yarn**
**paper punch**
**scissors**

> *Ahead of time:*
> • Photocopy Joseph and the pit.
> • Cut yarn into 18-inch lengths.

## Group time:

- Ask the children to stand up if they have a brother or sister.
- Ask: What do you like best about having a brother or sister? What do you like least?
- Read the story "Joseph's Bad Day."
- Ask: What did Joseph do that made him so unlikeable? Do you think you would have liked to have Joseph for a brother? Why or why not? Was dumping him in a dry well a good solution to the problem?
- Create the action story picture.

## ACTION STORY PICTURE

1. Color and cut out Joseph and the wall of the pit.
2. Glue the wall to a business-sized envelope.
3. Punch holes on the circles near the top and bottom and thread the yarn through.
4. Tie the yarn on the back of the envelope as shown.
5. Fold "Joseph" over the yarn. Glue the front and back together with the yarn inside.
6. Pull the yarn up and down from the back to raise and lower Joseph from the pit.

21

# Joseph and the King

**Bible Story**
Genesis 39–46

**Bible Verse**
You didn't send me here; it was God.
  Genesis 45:8, CEB

**Green Message**
God can use each of us to do good in the world.

Joseph, Jacob's beloved son, was taken to Egypt where he was sold as a slave. An officer in the king's army bought him and took him to his home. Joseph worked very hard. But he missed his father, he missed his home, he missed his brothers.

One day the officer's wife accused Joseph of doing something wrong. He was innocent, but they threw him into prison. Joseph was scared. But Joseph continued to work very hard and do the best he could. God had not forgotten Joseph.

The prisoners soon discovered that Joseph had a special gift. Joseph could tell people what their dreams meant. They would come to him and Joseph would help them.

The king of Egypt was having bad dreams. One of his servants who had been in prison remembered Joseph and his gift. He told the king about him. The king had Joseph brought to him. "Let me tell you about my dreams," said the king.

Joseph said, "God is sending you a message. There will be seven years when food will be plentiful. There will be seven years when nothing will grow. You must store up food during the good years to feed the people during the bad years."

The king put Joseph in charge of collecting grain. When the seven bad years came, Egypt was prepared. But other countries were not so lucky.

One day Joseph's brothers came to buy grain. They did not recognize Joseph. So Joseph decided to trick them. He called them spies and threatened to put them in jail. He even had Simeon arrested. Joseph sent them home and told them to bring their younger brother Benjamin back with them.

When the food ran out, the brothers had to come back—with Benjamin—to get more grain. This time Joseph hid his silver cup in Benjamin's sack of grain. When the brothers tried to leave, Joseph arrested Benjamin. The other brothers offered to take his place. Joseph knew then that they had changed. He told them who he was and sent them home to bring their father back to Egypt to live.

## Supplies ......................................................

| | | |
|---|---|---|
| plastic containers (16-oz. margarine, 6-oz. yogurt) | glitter | rick-rack |
| | paper plate (for glitter) | faux gemstones |
| | plastic tub or dishpan | scraps of metallic trim |
| craft glue or glue gun | silver spray paint | recycled newspaper |

## Ahead of time:

- Spray paint the plastic containers with metallic silver paint designed for plastics. Do this in a well-ventilated area. Allow them to dry overnight.
- Pour glitter onto a paper plate. Set the plate inside a plastic tub or dishpan.

## Group time:

- Ask: What do you think it would be like to be far away from your home and family where you didn't know anyone?
- Tell the story "Joseph and the King."
- Ask: What was Joseph's special gift? How did he use this gift to help other people? How did Joseph turn something bad into something good?

- Make Joseph's silver cup.
- Select one cup to be used in the game. Begin music and let the children pass the cup around the circle. Stop the music. Whoever is holding the cup has to tell something about the story of Joseph.

### JOSEPH'S SILVER CUP

1. Glue the larger container and smaller container together, forming a chalice.
2. Use scraps of metallic trim, ribbon, rick-rack, and faux gemstones to decorate the cup.
3. Run a bead of white glue along the upper edge of the chalice.
4. Dip the rim into the glitter. Shake any excess glitter back onto the plate.
5. Cut out the Bible verse below and glue it inside the larger container.

> # You didn't send me here; it was God.
> ### Genesis 45:8, CEB

# A Baby in a Basket

**Bible Story**
Exodus 2:1-10

**Bible Verse**
God cares for you.
  1 Peter 5:7, CEV

**Green Message**
God provides people
who love and care
for us.

The time of Joseph was long in the past. A new king came to power in Egypt. He did not like the Hebrew people. He was afraid of them. So he passed laws that would keep them from having children so their number would not grow.

But the laws did not stop families from having babies. One family had a little baby. They decided to hide him so that the king and his soldiers would not find him. But as most babies do, their son kept growing. Soon, he was too big to hide.

The mother wove a basket from dried reeds. It was just big enough for one tiny baby. She painted the outside with tar so that it would float. She put warm blankets inside. Then she and her daughter Miriam took the basket to the river.

The mother placed the basket on the water. She kissed her baby and placed him inside. "Be quiet, my sweet boy. May God keep you safe from the wicked king," she said. "Miriam, stay here and keep watch. Make sure nothing happens to him."

Miriam scrunched down in the reeds so that she could see and yet not be seen. And she watched. Suddenly, she heard voices. It was the princess and her servants. They had come to the river to bathe. Miriam was worried.

One of the servants spotted the little basket and waded into the river to get it. She brought it to the princess who looked inside. "It's a baby. He must be one of the Hebrew babies. My father's law is so cruel. I will take this baby back with me to the palace. I will keep him safe. I will name him Moses."

Suddenly, Miriam knew what to do. She jumped up from her hiding place and ran to the princess. "I know someone who could help you care for him. Shall I get her?" Miriam ran back to the house and brought her mother to the princess.

God had kept her brother safe. Now Moses would grow up in the palace with his own mother taking care of him.

## Supplies

• • • • • • • • • • • • • • • • • • • • • • • • • • • • • • • • • • • • • • • • • •

15-oz. soup cans
paintbrushes
fabric scraps
scissors

white craft glue
water
small containers
recycled newspaper

small wooden beads,
  4 per child (optional)

## Ahead of time:

• Photocopy the directions for making the pencil holders and "Thank you" strip.

## Group time:

• Ask the children to identify the different people who take care of them each day. List them on a piece of paper.
• Point out to them that God provides people who will love and care for us because God loves and cares for us.

• Read "A Baby in a Basket."
• Ask: Why did Moses' mother put him in a basket and place the basket in the river? Who were the different people who took care of him?
• Make a thank-you gift for a caregiver.

- - - - - - - - - - - - - - - - - - - - - - - - - - - - - - - - - - - - - - - - ✂

### PENCIL HOLDER GIFT

1. Mix together equal parts of white craft glue and water. Mixture should be paintable but not too thin.
2. Cover the work surface with newspaper.
3. Start anywhere on the can. Paint a small amount of glue mixture onto the surface. Apply a fabric scrap. Then paint more of the glue mixture over the top of the fabric and smooth it out.
4. Repeat this process, overlapping the fabric scraps so that none of the can's surface shows through.

5. Use scissors to trim any pieces of fabric that are sticking out above the can.
6. Cut out the strip that says "Thank You."
7. Using the same process, "paint" the words onto the can.
8. Let dry completely before using.

HINT: *Start at the top and work to the bottom. Fold the edges of the scraps under the can.*

COOL OPTION: *Glue four wooden beads that are the same size to the bottom for "feet."*

Thank You!

# A Call From God

**Bible Story**
Exodus 2:11–3:22, 27

**Bible Verse**
I will be with you.
  Exodus 3:12, CEV

**Green Message**
God promises to help us even when he asks us to do difficult things.

Moses grew up in the palace, but he never forgot his own people. But one day Moses committed a terrible crime. His temper got the better of him. So he had to leave the only land he had ever known.

Moses ran far, far away from Egypt. He stayed with a man named Jethro. Moses worked for Jethro, taking care of his sheep. Moses even married Jethro's daughter. He lived there for many years. Everything was good. Moses had almost forgotten about Egypt. Then one day something strange happened.

While Moses was out watching Jethro's sheep, he saw a bush on the hillside that was burning. It was a very odd fire, because even though the flames leaped up high, the bush was not being burned up. *What kind of a fire does that?* Moses decided to look and see for himself.

As Moses came near the bush, he heard a voice coming from inside the bush. "Moses! Don't come any closer. Take off your shoes. You are standing on holy ground."

*"What's going on?"* Moses wondered. *"A voice coming from a bush? Holy ground? Who is this? What does all this mean?"*

Then the voice said, "I am the God of your father, the God of Abraham, the God of Isaac, and the God of Jacob. I have heard my people crying out in Egypt. They are tired of being slaves. It is time for them to leave. You are the one I have chosen to help them."

Moses thought to himself, *"Go back to Egypt? Face the king after all I have done? This is not a good idea."* Out loud Moses asked, "Are you sure it is me that you want?"

"You will lead my people out of Egypt. You can do it because I will be with you. I will teach you what to say. I will send your brother Aaron to help you. I am God. You will see what I can do."

Moses set out for Egypt. Along the way he ran into his brother Aaron who had been sent to meet him. Moses knew then that God's plan was underway, and it could not fail.

## Supplies

corrugated cardboard
lunch-sized paper bags
masking tape
crayons or markers

art tissue (green, red, yellow, orange)
small containers
white glue

scissors
glue sticks

## Ahead of time:

- Open up the paper bags. Remove the bottom from each bag.
- Cut cardboard into 8-inch squares.
- Photocopy the figure and directions for each child.

## Group time:

- Ask: Have you ever been asked to do something that was very, very hard? How did you feel? Did you do it? Did you have help?
- Read "A Call From God."
- Ask: Have you ever felt that God was calling you to do something? *(Invite the children to share.)*
- Ask: What did Moses say to God? What did you learn from the story of Moses?
- Make the burning bush.

### BURNING BUSH

1. Gather the bottom of the paper bag, spreading it out to form the base of the trunk as shown.
2. Pinch and twist the trunk area together until it holds on its own.
3. Spread white glue in a circle in the center of a cardboard square.
4. Press the base of the trunk onto the glue. Hold in place with masking tape until dry.
5. Cut 4-inch strips of red, orange, green, and yellow art tissue for leaves and flames.
6. Make three slits from the top of the trunk down about six inches.
7. Twist each of the four sections tightly to form the branches.
8. Twist each tissue strip in the center, then dip the center into white glue. Press the strips onto the branches of the bush.
9. Color and cut out the figure of Moses.
10. Put glue between the two sides of the figure and press, leaving the tabs free.
11. Fold up the tabs and glue them to the cardboard. *(The sandals will be on the ground beside Moses.)*

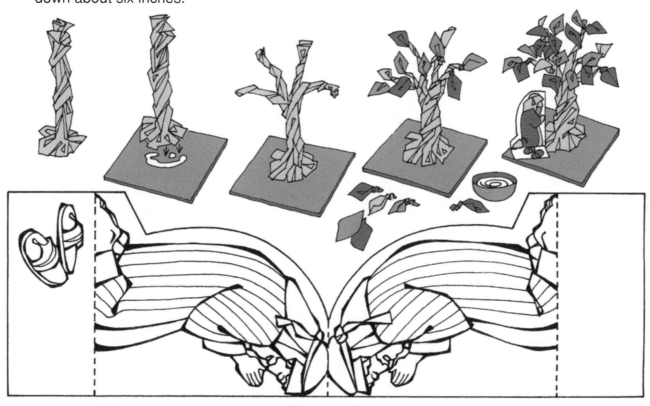

# Let My People Go!

### Bible Story
Exodus 6:10–12:39

### Bible Verse
You are wonderful, LORD, and you deserve all praise.
  Psalm 145:3, CEV

### Green Message
God is more powerful than we can possibly imagine.

God gave Aaron and Moses a job: Free my people! So that is what they set out to do. Over hill and down through valleys, Aaron and Moses traveled until they came to the palace of the king of Egypt. "We have a message from God," said Moses to the king. "Our God says, 'Let my people go!' If you don't, terrible things are going to happen to your people."

The king was not impressed. "Who are you? Who is your God? Why should I pay any attention to you at all? And just because you are standing here making these dumb demands, I will make your people work even harder!" Moses and Aaron left the palace. The king made the people work even harder than before, just as he had said.

Then Moses and Aaron went back to the palace. "If you don't let God's people go, then God will turn the water in the river into blood. There will not be a drop of water to drink anywhere in the land."

But the king was not convinced. "I don't believe you can do that!" Aaron went to the edge of the river. He touched the water with his staff. The water turned red, red as blood.

"OK, OK," said the king, "When the water becomes water again, I will let your people go."

But the king did not let the people go. "I can't do the work I need to do if I don't have workers. I've decided not to let the people go. Go away. Don't come back."

But Moses and Aaron did come back. They came back many times. This king was stubborn. Next God sent frogs. Then God sent flies and grasshoppers and sickness and darkness. Each time the king said "Go," and each time the king changed his mind.

Finally God was tired of the king's attitude. So God sent the angel of death to walk the streets of Egypt. The king was finally convinced. "Go! Take your people and leave! Take what you want with you. Just leave!" he shouted.

And God's people left.

## Supplies ● ● ● ● ● ● ● ● ● ● ● ● ● ● ● ● ● ● ● ● ● ● ● ● ● ● ● ● ● ● ●

| | | |
|---|---|---|
| **paper fasteners** | **plastic pudding cups** | **clear tape** |
| **string or crochet thread** | **cellulose sponges** | **crayons or markers** |
| **utility knife (adult only)** | **water** | **scissors** |

## Ahead of time:

- Photocopy the croaking frog and directions.
- Cut the string into 24-inch lengths.
- Poke a hole in the bottom of each pudding cup with a utility knife.
- Cut sponges crosswise into four pieces. Each child needs one piece.

## Group time:

- Make the croaking frogs.
- Ask: Have you ever tried to convince someone of something, but they just didn't listen? What did you do to convince them?
- Read "Let My People Go!" Whenever the king changes his mind, have the children make their frogs croak.
- Ask: What were the reasons the king gave for not allowing the people to leave? How would you have felt if you were Moses or Aaron? How would you have felt if you were God? What finally convinced the king?

## CROAKING FROG

1. Wrap one end of the string around a paper fastener several times and tie in a knot.
2. Push the fastener (from the inside of the cup to the outside) through the hole in the bottom of the cup.
3. Spread the arms of the fastener out across the bottom of the cup. (The head of the paper fastener will be inside the cup. The string will hang down below the cup.)
4. Color and cut out Fred the Frog.
5. Using clear tape, attach the frog to the cup as shown here.
6. Dampen the sponge slightly.
7. Hold the cup in one hand. Wrap a piece of sponge around the string. When you pull the sponge down the string with a jerking motion, Fred will croak.

# Are We There Yet?

**Bible Story**
Exodus 16:1-17:7

**Bible Verse**
O taste and see that
the LORD is good.
   Psalm 34:8, NRSV

**Green Message**
God provides what we
need when we need it.

With God's help, Moses led the people into the wilderness toward the land God promised. They traveled for days and days and months and months. Soon the food and water they had brought with them ran out.

**Moses, Moses, we're so sad. We're tired, we're hungry, and the water tastes bad. Are we there yet?**

God led the people to a place where there was water. God showed Moses how to throw a special tree branch into the water to make it taste better.

**Moses, Moses, we're just dead. We've walked for weeks, and we want some bread. Are we there yet?**

God sent the people a special food. It was called manna. It lay on the ground like frost and tasted like biscuits made with honey.

**Moses, Moses, we're just beat. We've got no homes and we want some meat. Are we there yet?**

The next day God sent a flock of quail to the people. The quail had been flying so long, they were tired and easy to catch. That night the people had a delicious quail stew.

**Moses, Moses, it's getting hotter. We're tired and thirsty, and we want some water. Are we there yet?**

God had Moses strike a rock with his staff. Water gushed forth. The people filled their jars to overflowing.

Moses asked the people, "Is there anything *else* you need? You have bread in the morning and meat at night. There is sweet, cool water gushing from the stones. God has provided *everything* you could possibly need."

"There is just one more thing we'd like to ask," the people said to Moses.

**All: "Are we there yet?"**

## Supplies ·····························

**crayons or markers**
**scissors**
**craft glue**

**old advertisements or calendars**
 **with magnetic backing (see p. 32)**
**old file folders**

## Ahead of time:

- Photocopy a set of the Funky Fruits and Vegetables for each child.
- Cut refrigerator magnet ads or calendars into 1-inch squares, six per set.

## Group time:

- Ask: What is your favorite food? What is your favorite fruit? vegetable? snack food? Where do you get your food?
- Read "Are We There Yet?"
- Ask: What did the people want Moses to do? Why do you think Moses became annoyed with the people? Did God provide what the people needed?
- Make the Funky Fruits and Vegetables.
- Remind the children that God knows what they need and God cares about them.

• • • • • • • • • • • • • • • • • • • • • • • • • • • • • • • • • • • • • • • • • • • • • ✂

## FUNKY FRUIT AND VEGETABLE MAGNETS

1. Color the Funky Fruits and Vegetables.
2. Cut them out and glue them to scraps of cardboard (such as old file folders).
3. Glue one magnet piece to the back of each figure. (Make sure the glue goes on the side that has writing on it.)
4. Put your magnets on the refrigerator at home to remind you that God provides us with good foods to eat.

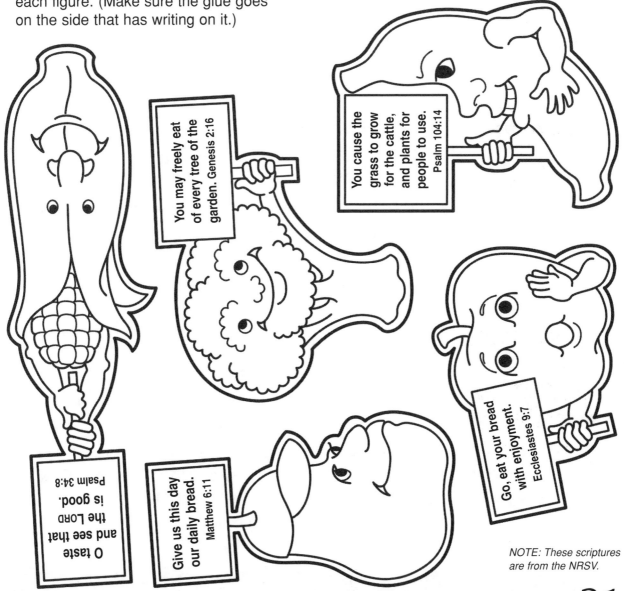

You may freely eat of every tree of the garden. Genesis 2:16

You cause the grass to grow for the cattle, and plants for people to use. Psalm 104:14

Go, eat your bread with enjoyment. Ecclesiastes 9:7

O taste and see that the Lord is good. Psalm 34:8

Give us this day our daily bread. Matthew 6:11

*NOTE: These scriptures are from the NRSV.*

*31*

# God's Top Ten

**Bible Story**
Exodus 20:1-17

**Bible Verse**
I treasure your word in my heart.
  Psalm 119:11, NRSV

**Green Message**
God's laws help us know how to love God and how to treat one another.

When Moses and the people came to the base of Mount Sinai, God said to Moses, "Come to the top of the mountain. I want to talk to you about the way I want the people to live." Moses climbed to the very top of the mountain. He was on the mountain for a long time. When he finally came down, he was carrying two stone tablets. "God has given us some rules to follow," said Moses. "These rules will help us know how to live."

**Rule #1:  You shall have no other gods before me.**

Moses said, "God should be the most important thing in our lives."

**Rule #2: You shall not bow down to idols and worship them.**

Moses said, "We should not worship things more than God."

**Rule #3: You shall not make wrongful use of the name of God.**

Moses said, "We should only use God's name respectfully."

**Rule #4: Keep the sabbath day holy.**

Moses said, "We should set aside one day each week for God."

**Rule #5: Honor your father and mother.**

Moses said, "God wants us to respect our parents."

**Rule #6: You shall not murder.**

Moses said, "God is unhappy whenever we hurt someone else."

**Rule #7: You shall be faithful to your husband or wife.**

Moses said, "God wants husbands and wives to be faithful."

**Rule #8: You shall not steal.**

Moses said, "God wants us to respect the possessions of others."

**Rule #9: You shall not lie.**

Moses said, "God wants us to always tell the truth."

**Rule #10: You shall not want what belongs to your neighbor.**

Moses said, "God wants us to be satisfied with what we have."

MAGNETIC ADVERTISEMENT

## Supplies • • • • • • • • • • • • • • • • • • • • • • • • • • • •

corrugated cardboard
magnetic spray paint
utility knife (adults only)
pencil

old advertisements or calendars
  with magnetic backing
scissors
craft glue

## Ahead of time:

- Photocopy the Ten Commandments Game.
- Cut corrugated cardboard into tablet shapes about 8- by 11-inches. (See photo below.)
- Spray paint each tablet with magnetic paint
- Cut refrigerator magnet ads or calendars into thin strips about three inches long.

NOTE: *Magnetic spray paint is lead free and cleans up with soap and water. It dries to the touch in about fifteen minutes and is available at most hardware stores.*

## Group time:

- Ask: What kind of rules do you have at home? at school? Why do you think we have rules? Did you know that God gave us rules?
- Read "God's Top Ten."
- Point out to the children that the first four commandments tell us how to love God. The next six tell us how to treat one another.
- Make the Ten Commandments game.

- - - - - - - - - - - - - - - - - - - - - - - - - - - - - - - - - - - - - - - ✂

### THE TEN COMMANDMENTS GAME

1. Cut out the strips below.
2. Put glue on the printed side of the magnet pieces and glue one to the back of each commandment strip.
3. See who can put them in order first.

| | |
|---|---|
| You shall have no other | gods before me. |
| You shall not bow down | to idols and worship them. |
| You shall not make wrongful | use of the name of God. |
| Keep the | sabbath day holy. |
| Honor your | father and mother. |
| You shall not | murder. |
| You shall be | faithful to your husband or wife. |
| You shall | not steal. |
| You | shall not lie. |
| You shall not want | what belongs to your neighbor. |

# The Walls of Jericho

**Bible Story**
Joshua 6

**Bible Verse**
Be strong and courageous...for the LORD your God is with you.
   Joshua 1:9, NRSV

**Green Message**
With God, nothing is impossible.

For forty years God's people had no home of their own. They were tired. They wanted the land that God had promised to them. Finally, God told Moses that the time had finally come.

Moses said, "I'm very old. I'm not strong enough to lead them."

"Moses, I have chosen a new leader for the people. His name is Joshua. He will listen to my words. He will lead the people. I will help him, just as I have helped you," said God.

So Joshua became the new leader. Joshua trusted God, but he was afraid. The people who lived in this new land were very strong. Their cities were protected and their armies were strong. They did not want God's people to live there.

"Joshua, everything will be OK if you will just do as I tell you," said God. "I will be with you just as I was with Moses."

Joshua called all the people together. "We have finally come to the land God promised. It is time for us to have a land of our own. The first city we will come to is the city of Jericho. Its walls are high and the gates will be locked. They do not want us to come there. But God will help us if we do just as God says."

Joshua said, "Here is the plan. For six days we will walk in silence around the city one time. Our priests will blow the trumpets and we will carry the special box with God's rules in it. Then on the seventh day we will walk around the city seven times. At the signal, everyone will shout. Watch what happens."

So Joshua led the people up to the walls of Jericho. They marched quietly around the city one time for six days. On the seventh day they marched around the city seven times. Then everyone shouted. What do you think happened? *(The walls fell down!)*

## Supplies ..........................................................

| | | |
| --- | --- | --- |
| **1-quart plastic milk bottles (clean, with labels removed)** | **utility knife (adult only)** **permanent marker** **colored tape** | **craft glue** **crayons or markers** **scissors** |

## Ahead of time:

- Photocopy "Joshua's Trumpets."
- Remove the bottoms of the milk containers.

## Group time:

- Make the trumpets.
- Read "The Walls of Jericho." When the time comes for the people to blow the trumpets, let the children march around the room and add the sound effects.

HINT: *Tape a permanent marker across the top edge of a book as shown below. Turn the bottle to make a perfectly level cutting line.*

- Talk with the children about how God's plan must have seemed impossible to Joshua.

✂

## JOSHUA'S TRUMPETS

1. Wrap a piece of colored masking tape, duct tape, or electrical tape around the bottom edge of the container to cover the rough edge.
2. Color and cut out the Bible verse.
3. Attach the verse to the container.
4. Wrap additional strips of the colored tape around the container as decoration.

Be strong and courageous...
for the LORD your God is with you.

---

# Be strong and
# courageous...
# for the LORD your God is with you.
## Joshua 1:9, NRSV

# Deborah Fights for God

### Bible Story
Judges 4:4-16

### Bible Verse
You are my God.
Show me what you
want me to do.
  Psalm 143:10, CEV

### Green Message
We should trust the
power of God.

A long time ago in the land of God's people, the people were ruled by judges instead of kings. Judges helped the people know what they were supposed to do. One such judge was named Deborah. She was more than just a judge. She knew the word of God. She talked to God. God told her what to do.

One day some soldiers came to General Barak. "Our people are in trouble. We need to do something!"

"I don't know what to do," said the general. "Our army is strong, but we are small. We are no match for our enemies."

"Are we supposed to sit back and watch them ruin our crops and steal our animals?" asked the soldiers.

"But their army has iron chariots pulled by strong horses," said the general. "We can't compete with that!"

"If you don't know what to do, then maybe you should ask Deborah to help us," said the soldier." Maybe God will tell her what YOU should do."

So General Barak went to see Deborah. When he got there, he found that Deborah had a message for him. "God wants you to take ten thousand soldiers and go up the mountain. At a certain time, you will march down the mountain and defeat the enemy."

"You make it sound so easy," said General Barak. "But you won't be the one facing those iron chariots."

"God will give you the victory," said Deborah.

"If you are so certain of that, then stand next to me on the battlefield," said the general.

So Deborah went to battle with General Barak and the army. She trusted the power of God and helped lead the army to victory.

## Supplies ••••••••••••••••••••••••••••••••••••••••••••••

| corrugated cardboard | compass or circle pattern | scissors |
| utility knife (adult only) | silver duct tape | craft glue |

## Ahead of time:
- Photocopy the directions and shield center.
- Cut cardboard into 18-inch circles.

## Group time:
- Read "Deborah Fights for God."
- Talk with the children about the importance of trusting God in difficult situations.
- Make Deborah's shield.
- Point out to the children that God's people discovered that they didn't really need a great army. All they needed was God.

• • • • • • • • • • • • • • • • • • • • • • • • • • • • • • • • • • • • • • • ✂

### DEBORAH'S SHIELD

1. Cover the front surface of the cardboard circle with duct tape. Start at the center and go to the outside edge. Tuck the ends to the back side.
2. When the front of the shield is completely covered, glue the Bible verse in the center.
3. Cut two eighteen-inch strips of duct tape.
4. Overlap the strips slightly, creating a strip eighteen inches long and about three inches wide.
5. Turn the strip sticky side up.
6. Fold the tape over itself as shown below. Leave three inches at either end unfolded.
7. Attach the sticky ends to the back of the shield as shown. This is the handle for the shield.

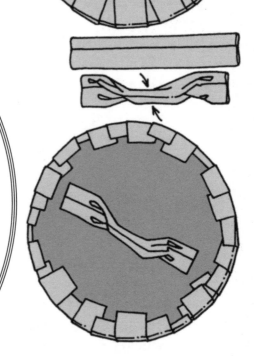

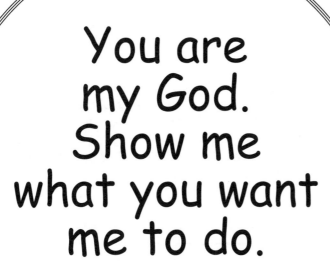

You are
my God.
Show me
what you want
me to do.

Psalm 143:10, CEV

# Ruth's New Family

**Bible Story**
Book of Ruth

**Bible Verse**
May the LORD reward you for your deeds.
Ruth 2:12, CEB

**Green Message**
God sees our unselfish acts of kindness and is pleased.

Rain had not fallen in Israel for a long, long time. Harvest came but there was nothing to pick. Many families moved to other lands where there was food to eat. They left their homes and their friends behind. But God was with them in their new land.

Naomi and her husband and their sons built a home in this new land. But one day Naomi's husband grew ill and died. Naomi wondered who would look after her and help her.

"Don't worry, mother," said her sons. "We have families of our own now. We will take care of you."

Naomi loved her sons and their wives. They had a happy life. But Naomi's happiness did not last very long. One day, both of her sons became ill and died.

"Now what will I do?" Naomi asked. "There is no one to take care of us. I am going back to my old home to live. Life is better there now." Then Naomi told her two daughters-in-law her plans.

"Let us go with you," the two young women said.

"Stay here in your own land where you will be happy. Maybe you will find husbands and have new families," said Naomi.

Orpah kissed her mother-in-law and went back to her family. But Ruth decided to stay with Naomi. "I will go with you. I will take care of you. You will need help. You will not be alone."

Naomi and Ruth set off for Israel. When they arrived at Naomi's old home, the people of the village rushed out to greet them. They were happy to see Naomi and they welcomed Ruth as well.

Ruth kept her promise. Every day she went into the fields and gathered grain for she and Naomi. The owner of the field saw how hard she worked. He also saw how kind she was. Boaz offered to marry Ruth. They would be a family for Naomi. When they had a child of their own, Naomi was so happy. She would never be alone again.

## Supplies ....................................................

- natural wheat stalks
- colored ribbon (8-inch lengths)
- recycled newspaper
- old towels

*Ahead of time:*
Soak the wheat stalks in a pan of water overnight, or at least for a couple of hours. A cookie sheet with a raised edge is perfect for these long stalks.

## Group time:

- Ask: Can you think of a time when everything seemed to be going wrong? What did you do? How did you feel?
- Read "Ruth's New Family."
- Ask: What are some of the things that happened to Naomi and her family?

- Ask: How did Ruth respond to her mother-in-law? Who noticed her kindness?
- Make special "Love Gifts" to share.

- - - - - - - - - - - - - - - - - - - - - - - - - - - - - - - - - - - - - - - - - ✂

### LOVE GIFTS

1. Cover the table with recycled newspaper and old towels.
2. With the ribbon, tie three wheat stalks together, just below the heads. (See the diagram.)
3. Braid the three stalks until you get close to the end. (Remove any extra leaves to make it easier.)

4. Bring the end of the braid up where you tied the heads together, forming a loop.
5. Tie a second knot with the ribbon, holding the end of the braided stalks in place. Tie a bow using the ribbon.
6. Trim the ends of the stalks and the ribbon.

In Bible times, men who worked in the fields would often make "love knots" out of the wheat for their wives or their potential wives. Boaz saw Ruth's acts of kindness and knew that she would be a wonderful wife. God rewards us for our acts of kindness toward others.

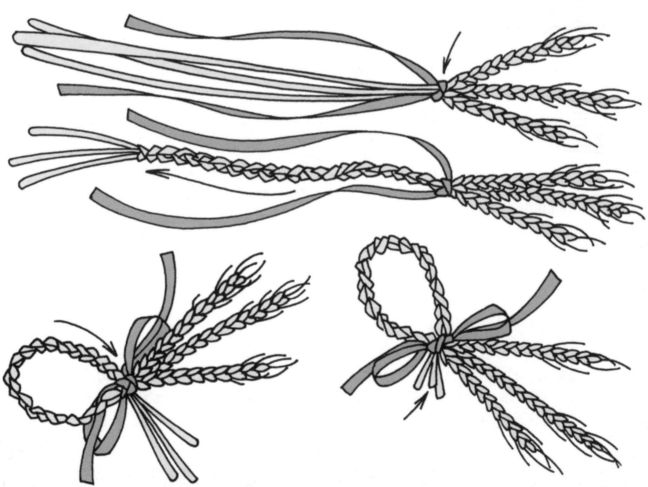

# Hannah's Prayer

**Bible Story**
1 Samuel 1:1–2:21

**Bible Verse**
Be gracious to me,
and hear my prayer.
  Psalm 4:1c, NRSV

**Green Message**
We can talk to God
anywhere about
anything.

---

**Pronunciation:**
Elkanah (el-KAY-nuh)

Long ago in Bible times, God set aside special days and special places for the people to worship God. These places of worship were not just down the street or right around the corner. People often had to travel for days to get there. Worship days were times of great celebration and excitement.

On one occasion, Elkanah and his family made the trip to the place of worship. While Elkanah was busy making offerings to God, his wife Hannah slipped into the place of prayer. She had a special request of her very own.

"Please, God," said Hannah. "Elkanah and I want to be a family. We would like a son to love and care for. If you will do this for me, I promise that as long as he lives, he will be your servant."

Over and over Hannah prayed the same prayer. If God didn't hear her the first time, maybe God would hear her the second or third or fourth time.

What Hannah did not know was that Eli, the priest of the temple was watching her. "Woman, you are making a scene. Stop it this very minute!"

"Oh, please, sir, I am asking God for something special. My husband and I would like a son," said Hannah.

"Go in peace. May God answer your prayer," said the priest.

Elkanah and Hannah returned to their home. Hannah felt that God had finally heard her prayer. The next year when the special days of worship came, Elkanah went to the temple by himself. He did this because he and Hannah had a brand new baby boy. His name was Samuel.

Elkanah and Hannah raised Samuel to love and serve God. When Samuel was old enough, Hannah brought him to the temple, just as she had promised.

## Supplies ..............................................

| | | |
|---|---|---|
| old advertisements or calendars with magnetic backing (See p. 32) | plastic lids (width 3-inches) pencils and scissors colored paper | old file folders photos of students craft glue |

## Ahead of time:

- Photocopy the magnet patterns and directions.
- Cut refrigerator magnet ads or calendars into 2-inch squares.
- Take individual pictures of the boys and girls in your group.

## Group time:

- Ask: When you talk to God, what do you say? Do you ever ask for anything special?
- Read "Hannah's Prayer."
- Ask: What did Hannah ask for?

- Ask: What did she promise to do in return? Did she keep her promise?
- Have the children make a magnet to share with their mother or stepmother.

✂

## FLOWER FRAME MAGNET

1. Press paper into the lid as shown. Remove and trim along the creased edge. Set aside.
2. Trace the outside of the lid onto an old file folder. Cut out to make the flower center.
3. Use the leaf pattern to cut two green leaves.
4. Use the petal pattern to cut eight petals in different colors.
5. Glue the leaves onto the flower center.
6. Glue the petals around the edge on top of the leaves. (Make sure the leaves still show. See illustration.)

7. Put glue on the bottom of the plastic lid and place it over the flower so that the petals and leaves are sandwiched beneath the lid.
8. Place a heavy book on top until the glue sets.
9. Use the guide created in Step 1 to trim a recent photograph of yourself so that it will fit inside the lid.
10. Put glue on the printed side of a magnet piece. Attach it to the back of the flower frame.

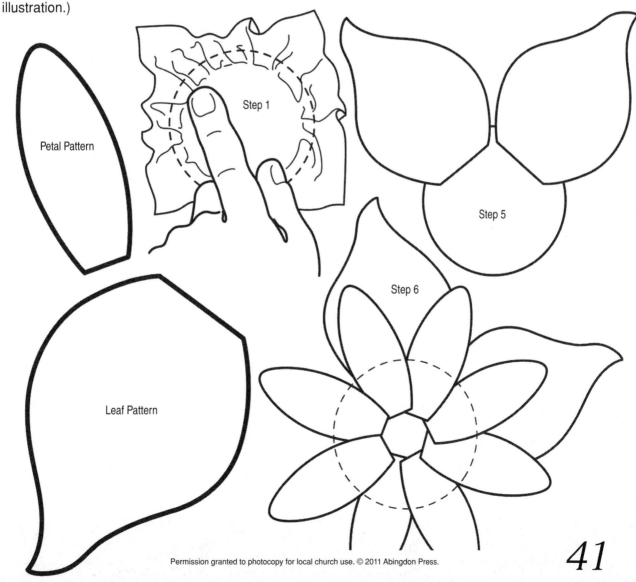

Petal Pattern

Step 1

Step 5

Step 6

Leaf Pattern

# Samuel! Samuel!

**Bible Story**
1 Samuel 3

**Bible Verse**
Speak, LORD, for your servant is listening.
 1 Samuel 3:9, NRSV

**Green Message**
Even though we may be young, God calls us to do important things.

Hannah never forgot her promise to God. When her son Samuel was old enough, she presented him to Eli, to serve God. Samuel helped around the temple. He filled all the lamps with oil. He opened the great doors. He did everything that Eli asked him to do.

One night Samuel was very tired and lay down on his mat. But just as he closed his eyes, he heard a voice. "Samuel! Samuel!" said the voice.

Samuel jumped up from his mat and ran to where Eli was sleeping. He knelt down and shook Eli. "Here I am Eli! What do you want?" he asked.

Eli sat up, rubbing his eyes. "What's the matter, Samuel?"

"You called me. What do you want?" said Samuel.

"I didn't call you. You must be dreaming. Go back to sleep," grumbled Eli, and Samuel walked back to his sleeping mat and lay back down. Soon he was fast asleep.

Just then Samuel heard the voice again. He jumped up from his mat and hurried to where Eli was sleeping. "Here I am Eli. What do you want?" asked Samuel.

Eli was confused. "I didn't call you, Samuel. Go back to bed."

Samuel went back to his mat. He wondered if he was imagining the voice. Just as Samuel's head touched the mat, he heard the voice a third time. A little more slowly, Samuel went to Eli.

"Eli, what do you want?" asked Samuel.

"Samuel, you are a good and obedient boy. But I didn't call you. I think I know who did. Go back to your mat. When you hear the voice again, say 'Speak, LORD, for your servant is listening.'" Samuel went back to his mat and lay down.

When the voice called a fourth time, Samuel didn't run to Eli. Instead he said, "Speak Lord, for your servant is listening." And that is how Samuel became a prophet of the Lord most high.

## Supplies ............................................

black construction
  paper (9 x 12 inches)

recycled magazines
scissors

glue sticks or tape
clear adhesive paper

## Ahead of time:
- Make a copy of the directions for Samuel's mat.
- To save time: Use a paper cutter to cut magazine pages into 1- by 10-inch strips.

## Group time:
- Read "Samuel! Samuel!" Invite two children to pantomime the action of the story as you read. One will be Samuel; the other Eli.
- Ask: What did Samuel do at the temple? Why was he there? Why didn't Samuel know who was calling him?
- Make Samuel's mat, similar to one he might have slept on at the temple. (Except that it would have been much larger.)

- - - - - - - - - - - - - - - - - - - - - - - - - - - - - - - - - - - - - - - - - ✂

### SAMUEL'S MAT

1. Choose about eight colorful strips from magazine pages.
2. Fold a sheet of 9- by 12-inch black construction paper in half sideways.
3. Make cuts across the fold to within one inch of the opposite edge. (See diagram.) Make the cuts curve and zigzag. Make some narrow and some wide.
4. Weave the strips of magazine pages through the cuts in the black construction paper.
5. Secure on the back with tape. Trim any overlaps.
6. Cover the front of the mat with clear adhesive paper so that it can be used as a placemat. Trim.

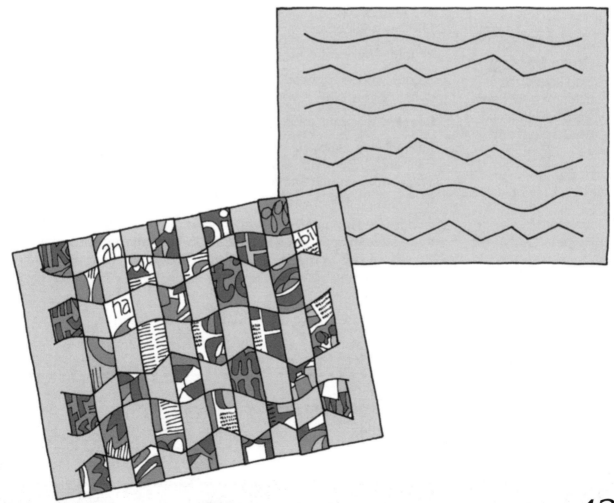

# A King for Israel

**Bible Story**
1 Samuel 8–10

**Bible Verse**
Just ask, and I will give you whatever you need.
 Psalm 81:10b, CEV

**Green Message**
God knows the difference between what we want and what we need.

Samuel served God for many years. He helped the people know what God wanted them to do. But Samuel was getting old and soon Israel would need a new leader.

The people looked at all the countries around them. These countries all had kings. So the people decided that they wanted a king too.

**People: We want a king! We want a king! We want a king!**

Samuel told them, "You don't want a king. A king will turn you into slaves. A king will make war on other countries. A king will turn your sons into soldiers."

**People: We want a king! We want a king! We want a king!**

Samuel said, "A king will take your money. A king will make you pay taxes on everything you own."

**People: We want a king! We want a king! We want a king!**

Samuel said, "You only think you want a king. You will get tired of a king. Then you will cry out to God to free you from this king. But God will not answer you."

**People: We want a king! We want a king! We want a king!**

Samuel shook his head. "You are ungrateful for all that God has done for you. God is your king. That should be enough for you."

**People: We want a king! We want a king! We want a king!**

Samuel was annoyed with the people. Samuel was angry with the people. But God said to Samuel, "Quit worrying about it. The people aren't rejecting you, they are rejecting me. I will help you choose a king for them."

God looked around for the right person to be the king. It had to be someone who was faithful to God. Finally, God decided. "I have chosen someone to be the king of my people. His name is Saul. As long as Saul follows my laws, then I will be with him and also with you."

**People: Yay! We have a king! Long live our king!**

## Supplies ••••••••••••••••••••••••••••••••••••••••••••••

**recycled foil gift wrap**  **glue sticks**
**stapler, staples**  **scissors**

## Ahead of time:
- Make a copy of the crown directions and the Bible verse.
- To speed up the process, pre-cut the strips of wrapping paper for both the crown base and the loops.

## Group time:
- Read "A King for Israel." Invite the children to be the people in the story.
- Ask: Why did the people want a king? Why do you think Samuel tried to discourage them? Did this make any difference?
- Make the crowns to wear.
- As the children work, talk about the differences between what we want and what we actually need.

- - - - - - - - - - - - - - - - - - - - - - - - - - - - - - - - - - - - - - - - ✂

## ROYAL CROWN

### Crown Base
1. Cut a piece of the foil wrapping paper eight inches deep and long enough to go around your head.
2. Lay the paper flat on the table.
3. Fold it down the middle, lengthwise. Open.
4. Fold the top edge down to meet the middle fold.
5. Fold the bottom edge up to meet the middle fold. (The two loose edges will be touching.)
6. Re-fold along the middle fold line with the loose edges to the inside.
7. Staple the ends together.

### Royal Loops
1. Cut ten pieces of foil wrapping paper eight inches long by six inches wide.
2. Prepare each piece the same as for the crown base. But bring the ends together to make a loop and staple.

3. Turn the crown base so that the loose edge (not the folded edge) is up.
4. Slip each loop into the base. Space them evenly.
5. Staple each loop.
6. Fit the crown to your head and staple.
7. Glue the Bible verse to the crown base. Imagine what it would be like to be king. What would you do with your power?

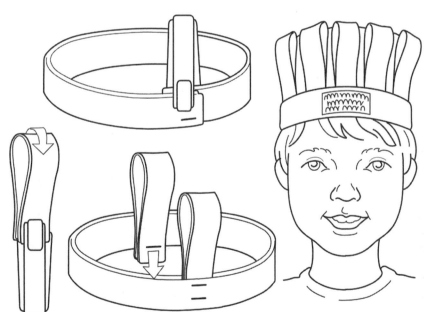

---

# Just ask, and I will give you whatever you need.
## Psalm 81:10b, CEV

# God Chooses David

**Bible Story**
1 Samuel 16:1-13

**Bible Verse**
The LORD looks on the heart.
  1 Samuel 16:7b, NRSV

**Green Message**
God knows who we are on the outside and the inside.

When Saul became the first king of Israel, he made a promise to follow God's commandments and obey God at all times. God promised Saul to always be with him and protect him and the people from their enemies. But like many promises that Saul made, he broke his promise to God.

God decided to choose someone else to be king. God wanted someone who would be faithful and obedient. "Samuel," said God, "I have chosen a new king. This new king lives with his family in the town of Bethlehem. Go there and anoint him."

Samuel set out for Bethlehem in secret. He did not want the king to know where he was going. When Samuel got to Bethlehem, he went to the home of Jesse and his family. "Jesse, God has chosen one of your sons to be the next king of Israel. Bring everyone together. God will tell me which one it is."

One by one, Jesse's sons stood in front of Samuel. After each one, Samuel asked God, "Is this the one? He is strong and handsome. He would make a wonderful king."

But God said to Samuel, "I do not look at people the way you do. I look at what is in their heart. It is none of these young men."

Samuel turned to Jesse, "Do you have any other sons?"

"My youngest son, David. He is out in the field watching the sheep," said Jesse. He sent a servant to bring David to them.

When David stood before Samuel, God said. "This is the one I have chosen. Anoint him, now."

Samuel poured the oil over David's head. From that day forward, God's spirit filled David and stayed with him forever. David would be the next king of Israel. But Saul was king right now. When would this be?

## Supplies ·······························

scissors
craft glue
glue sticks

red crayons
rubber bands
paper punch

plastic lids (5 inches)
recycled magazines

## *Ahead of time:*

• Make a copy of the directions for the "What's In Your Heart?" spinner.

## *Group time:*

• Ask: How do you know if a person is a good person or a not so good person? Can you tell by looking at their hair? their clothing? their shoes? How do you know?
• Read "God Chooses David."

• Ask: Who knows who we are on the outside as well as the inside? (God)
• Make the spinner. Have the children notice how the words that tell about themselves show up in the red heart.

• • • • • • • • • • • • • • • • • • • • • • • • • • • • • • • • • • • • • • • • • • • • ✂

### "WHAT'S IN YOUR HEART?" SPINNER

1. Cut out the two circles. Color the heart red.
2. Glue the heart circle to one side of the plastic lid.
3. Go through old magazines and find words that tell about you.
4. Cut out the words and glue them inside the second circle.
5. Glue the second circle to the other side of the plastic lid.
6. Punch two holes in the edge of the plastic lid, opposite each other as shown here.

7. Attach the rubber bands as shown here.
8. Hold the ends of the rubber bands. Twist back and forth, causing the lid to spin.

What happens when the disc spins?

REMEMBER: *God knows who you are on the outside and the inside.*

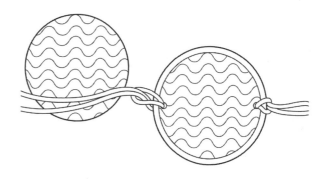

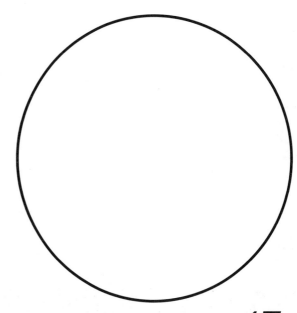

# David Praises God

### Bible Story
1 Samuel 16:14-23

### Bible Verse
Praise God with trumpets and all kinds of harps.
   Psalm 150:3, CEV

### Green Message
We should always praise God and give thanks.

King Saul did not know that that God had chosen a new king. But inside he felt it. Inside, King Saul felt angry all the time. Sometimes his feelings would show on the outside. He would yell. Sometimes he would throw things. No one wanted to be around him.

"King Saul, you are not yourself. How can we help you?" asked one of the king's servants.

"Help me? How CAN you help me? You are just servants. How can anyone help me?" the king demanded.

"Quiet music might help you feel better," suggested the servant. "I know someone who is very good at playing the harp. Maybe he could come to the palace and play for you." The servant had heard that David, the son of Jesse, was an excellent musician. He wrote songs of praise to God and would often sing them to his sheep to keep them calm.

"*Hmm.* Quiet music. That sounds good. I think I'd like that. He'd better be good. I don't want any loud music or wrong notes. That would not be very soothing," said the king almost pleasantly.

So the servants sent word to Jesse in Bethlehem. They told him to send his son David to the palace at once. Jesse was pleased that King Saul would invite his son to come to the palace.

The servants presented David to the king who said, "My spirit is troubled. I need something to make me feel better. Do you think you can help?"

"I will try, O King. You are God's chosen one. It is my duty to serve you," said David. King Saul liked David very much. He sent a message to Jesse asking if David could stay with him. Whenever the king was troubled, he would call for David and David would play for him. God was with David and blessed him. David in turn blessed King Saul with beautiful music and songs of praise.

## Supplies ••••••••••••••••••••••••••••••••••••••••••••

**scissors**               **crayons or markers**        **shallow boxes or box lids**
**glue sticks**            **rubber bands**                **(greeting card boxes)**

## Ahead of time:

- Make a copy of the directions and the Bible verse sheep.
- Bring in a variety of musical instruments and CD's to play for the children.

## Group time:

- Ask: What is your favorite kind of music?
- Play different styles of music, some loud and bouncy, some quiet and soothing.
- Ask: Which one would you rather listen to when you are working? when you are sleeping?
- Read "David Praises God."
- Ask: What instrument did David play?

- Ask: Do any of you play an instrument? Did you know that your voice is also an instrument?
- Remind the children that many of the songs that David wrote can be found in the Bible in a book called "Psalms."
- Ask: How was David's music a gift to King Saul?

• • • • • • • • • • • • • • • • • • • • • • • • • • • • • • • • • • • • • • • • • • • • ✂

### BOX HARP

1. Cut out the Bible verse sheep below.
2. Glue the sheep on the inside bottom of the box (or box lid) that you will be using.
3. Stretch four or five rubber bands over the box as shown here.
4. Strum the rubber bands. If the sound is too discordant, switch out different size bands.

David was in charge of his family's sheep. As a shepherd he would play the harp and sing to the sheep in order to keep them calm.

What kind of music would you play to make the king feel better?

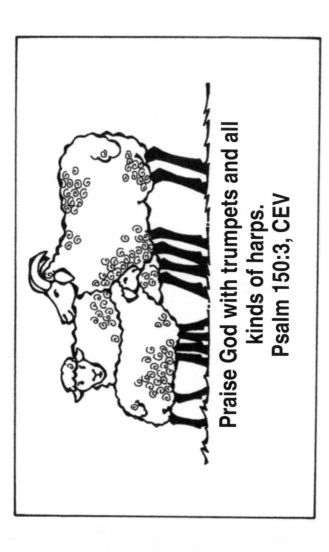

Praise God with trumpets and all kinds of harps. Psalm 150:3, CEV

# Solomon, the Wise King

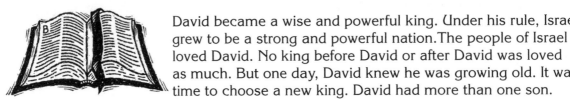

**Bible Story**
1 Kings 3

David became a wise and powerful king. Under his rule, Israel grew to be a strong and powerful nation. The people of Israel loved David. No king before David or after David was loved as much. But one day, David knew he was growing old. It was time to choose a new king. David had more than one son. Which son would he choose?

Finally, David chose his son Solomon to be the next king of Israel. David called Solomon to come to him. David wanted to tell him how to be a good king. "Solomon," said David, "I am getting old. There are many things I want to teach you about being a good king."

**Bible Verse**
Please make me wise and teach me the difference between right and wrong.
        1 Kings 3:9, CEV

Solomon knelt at his father's bedside, "Father, I want to be as good a king as you have been."

"Being a king is not easy. When bad things happen, and they will, ask for God to help you. Trust God and do whatever God tells you to do. Obey all of God's commandments. Turn to God to know what to do at all times."

When David died, Solomon took the throne. One night God came to Solomon in a dream. "What shall I give you?" asked God.

**Green Message**
It is better to be wise than to be rich.

"You were kind to my father David because he followed your laws and was faithful. I have only one request. Give me understanding that I might govern your people wisely."

God was pleased with Solomon. So God granted Solomon's request. God gave Solomon a great mind. Throughout all history, King Solomon was known for his great wisdom and understanding.

In addition, God also gave Solomon riches and power and long life. God also promised to be with Solomon and bless him as long as he walked in the ways of God.

## Supplies ·····································

plastic lids (large margarine or whipped topping tubs)
recycled paper grocery bags
scissors

crayons or markers
pencils
yarn

## Ahead of time:
• Photocopy the directions and patterns for the owl.

## Group time:
• Ask: What does it mean to be wise? Can you give me an example of what a wise saying or wise action would be? Did you know that there was once a king who was known to be very wise?
• Read "Solomon, the Wise King."

• Ask: When Solomon became the king, how did he become wise? When God asked him what gift he would choose, what things could he have asked for? What did God give him in addition to wisdom?
• Make the hanging owl.

- - - - - - - - - - - - - - - - - - - - - - - - - - - - - - - - - - - - - - - - - - - - - - - - - - ✂

**PRAYER OWL**

1. Trace around the plastic lid on a recycled paper grocery bag. Cut out.
2. Press the circle into the lid, running your finger around the inside edge. This will create an outline of the inside circle. Remove and trim.
3. Glue the circle in place in the lid.
4. Color and cut out the beak and eyes. Glue onto the circle.

5. Trace the wings, feet, and head feathers on a recycled paper grocery bag. Cut out.
6. Tape the wings, head feathers, and feet to the lid as shown here.
7. Tie a knot in a loop of yarn and tape to the back for hanging as shown.

An owl is considered to be wise. This owl will remind you to choose your actions wisely.

Cut one... head feathers (place on fold)

Cut one... eyes and beak

Cut two... wings

Cut two... feet

# Elijah's Promise

### Bible Story
1 Kings 17:1-16

### Bible Verse
Great is the LORD, and greatly to be praised.
Psalm 145:3, NRSV

### Green Message
God wants us to share what we have with others.

Once there was a man named Elijah. He was a prophet for God. Prophets were men and women, chosen by God, to deliver God's messages to the people. God sent Elijah to tell the king that things had to change or there would be trouble.

But the king would not listen and ordered Elijah to leave. God sent a drought to the land. The rain stopped coming. Rivers and streams and wells dried up. Nothing would grow. The people cried out to the king to help them. Elijah was afraid, so he went into hiding. *(caw)*

Even though the drought came, God cared for Elijah. Every day God would send ravens to bring Elijah meat and bread. The ravens made sure that Elijah did not starve. *(caw)*

Months passed. The drought went on and on and on. God told Elijah to leave the place where he was hiding. God sent Elijah to find a certain widow and her son. There Elijah would be safe.

Elijah saw the widow out picking up sticks for firewood. He went up to her. "I am hungry and tired. I would love a drink of water and a small piece of bread. God said you would take care of me," said Elijah. *(caw)*

"Where have you been? Don't you know there is a drought? Nothing will grow. My son and I have just a small amount of flour and a tiny bit of oil. It is only enough for one last meal for us. Then we will surely starve. How can I feed you?" she asked.

"If you will use your flour and oil to make some bread for me, you will see that God will take care of you," said Elijah. "God can do wonderful things." *(caw)*

The widow used the last of her flour and oil to make bread for the three of them. The next day came and she made more bread. Then the next and the next and the oil and flour never ran out. She knew that Elijah was truly a man of God. *(caw)*

## Supplies .......................................................

**lunch-sized paper bags**
**scissors**
**construction paper**
(black, yellow)

**glue sticks**
**craft glue**
**plastic bottle caps**
**black crayons**

*Ahead of time:*
• Photocopy the raven puppet patterns and directions.

## Group time:

- Ask: Have you ever heard of someone in the Bible who was known as a prophet? What do you think a prophet does? (delivers God's message to the people) Do you think people always liked prophets?
- Make the raven puppets.

- As you tell the story of Elijah the prophet, point to the children at the designated times and let them make the sound of a raven.
- Tell the story "Elijah's Promise."
- Ask: What did God do because the widow was willing to share her smallest amount of food?

✂

### RAVEN BAG PUPPET

1. Cover the front side of the bag with black paper.
2. Use the patterns to cut the head and wings from black paper and the beak and feet from yellow paper. Add to the puppet as shown.
3. Cut out the eyes and glue them on bottle caps. Glue the bottle caps to the raven's head.

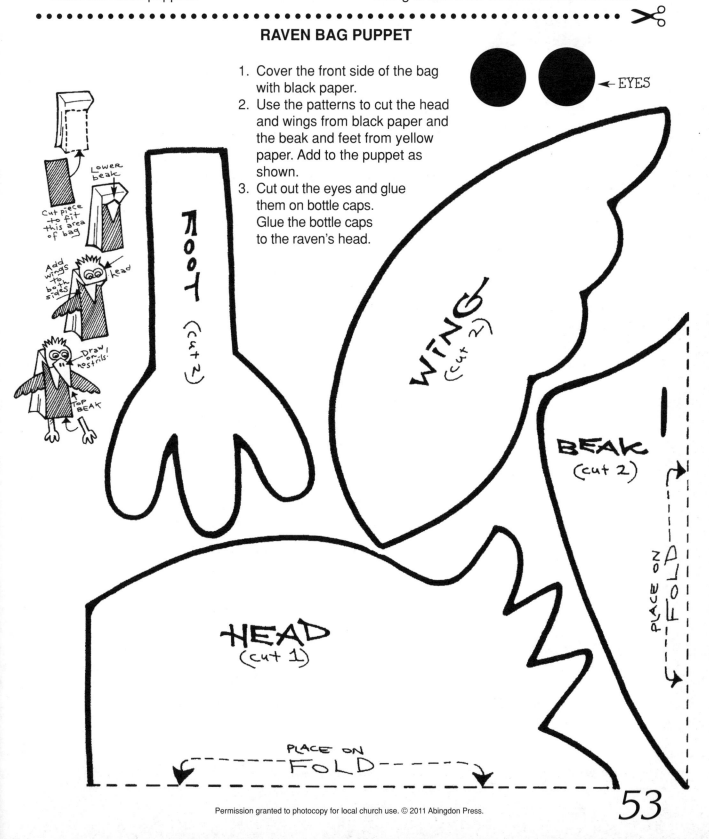

← EYES

LOWER beak

Cut piece to fit this area of bag

Add wings to both sides    head

Draw on nostrils

TOP BEAK

FOOT (cut 2)

WING (cut 2)

BEAK (cut 2)

PLACE ON FOLD

HEAD (cut 1)

PLACE ON FOLD

# Jars and Jars of Oil

## Bible Story
2 Kings 2:13-15; 4:1-7

## Bible Verse
Great is our Lord, and abundant in power.
    Psalm 147:5, NRSV

## Green Message
God's power is without measure.

Once there was a man whose name was Elisha. Elisha was one of God's prophets. Elisha delivered God's message to the people.

One day a poor widow came to Elisha. Her husband had just died and had left the family deep in debt. "I cannot pay our bills," the widow cried. "A creditor wants to take my two children as payment for the debt. Please help me!"

Elisha thought for a moment. How could he help this woman. "What do you have in your house?" he asked.

"That's the point. There is nothing in the house but a small jar of olive oil," said the widow.

"Go out to your neighbors and borrow as many jars as you can. Then I will tell you what to do with them."

The widow went from door to door, borrowing jars from everyone. Then she went back to Elisha. "My house is filled with empty jars," said the widow. "What shall I do now?"

"Go into your house and shut the door. Start pouring your oil into each jar. When one jar is full, set it aside and start another," said Elisha.

*Well, that won't last long. I have only one small jar of oil,* the widow thought to herself, but she went home and did as Elisha had told her.

When the first jar was almost filled, one of the boys brought his mother a second jar. Her tiny oil jar just kept pouring. "Look, Mama, there's still oil left in your jar." Soon every jar in the house was filled with oil.

"Now what do I do?" the widow asked Elisha.

"Sell the oil and pay off your debts. You and your children can live on the rest." And that is just what she did. God had performed a miracle through Elisha.

## Supplies ••••••••••••••••••••••••••••••••••••••••••••

used coffee grounds
cold coffee
flour and salt

measuring cup
large mixing bowl, spoon
wax paper

## Ahead of time:

- Photocopy the stone clay jar directions for each child.
- Mix up a recipe of the clay ahead of time to speed the process. Instead of air drying, you can microwave the jars in short bursts so the children may take them home today.

## Group time:

- Ask: When you are in trouble or in great need of help, who do you go to? Does God always answer your prayer in the way you expect?
- Read "Jars and Jars of Oil."

- Ask: How did God provide what the widow needed? Was it something that she expected? What did she discover about God?
- Make the stone clay jars.

✂ ⋯⋯⋯⋯⋯⋯⋯⋯⋯⋯⋯⋯⋯⋯⋯⋯⋯⋯⋯⋯⋯⋯⋯⋯

### STONE CLAY JARS

**Recipe for Stone Clay (Makes 5)**

    1 cup used coffee grounds
    1 cup flour
    ½ cup salt
    ½ cup cold coffee

TIP: *Used coffee grounds are necessary for the clay. Fresh ground coffee will make the clay crumbly and it will not harden.*

**How to Make the Jars**

1. In a large bowl, mix together the coffee grounds, the flour, and the salt.
2. Add the cold coffee a little at a time until the clay forms a molding consistency.
3. Give each child about ½ cup of the clay and let them mold a jar similar to one the widow might have provided. (HINT: *Start with a very fat snake as shown.*)
4. To harden, air dry overnight, bake at 325 degrees for about thirty minutes, or microwave in 10-second intervals.
5. When dry, the stone clay should have the look of a piece of ancient pottery.

COOL OPTION: *When dry, use acrylic poster paints to decorate the jar.*

roll out

smooth sides of jar

push thumb into clay to form opening

# A Burning Faith

**Bible Story**
Daniel 3:19-30

**Bible Verse**
Worship the Lord your God and serve only him.
Luke 4:8, CEB

**Green Message**
We are called to worship and serve God in everything we do.

---

**Pronunciation:**
Shadrach (SHAD-rak)
Meshach (MEE-shak)
Abednego (uh-BED ni-goh)

The King has built a statue and he said, "Bow low."
But three men drew the line. and they said, "Oh, no!"
**Shadrach, Meshach, Abednego.**

Now the king was very angry, and he told those three,
"You've gotta bow down or baked you'll be."
**Shadrach, Meshach, Abednego.**

But the three didn't budge, so they threw them in the fire,
While the flames in the furnace leaped higher and higher.
**Shadrach, Meshach, Abednego.**

And the guards who stood outside,
They were toasted to the bone.
But when the king looked inside,
He saw the three men weren't alone.
**Shadrach, Meshach, Abednego.**

When they pitched them in the furnace, there were only three.
But strolling through the flames you could clearly see,
**Shadrach, Meshach, Abednego.**

Another stood beside them in the fiery pit,
"I think it must be God, from the looks of it."
**Shadrach, Meshach, Abednego.**

When the king called them out not a single hair was burned.
"Your God has kept you safe, so freedom you have earned."
**Shadrach, Meshach, Abednego.**

"I know your God is great, much more powerful than me."

"Yes, God is our protector, you can clearly see,"
**Said Shadrach, Meshach, Abednego.**

## Supplies

| | | |
|---|---|---|
| utility knife (adult only) | permanent markers (red, yellow, orange and fine-tip black) | battery-operated tea lights |
| clean, quart-sized plastic milk bottles | | a whistle |
| scissors | chenille stems | tape |

## Ahead of time:

- Make a copy of "A Burning Faith" lantern directions, cut-outs, and Bible verse for each child.
- With a utility knife, cut one opening a little bigger than a battery-operated tea light on the back of each bottle near the bottom, and cut two holes at the top on either side.

## Group time:

- Say: Today we have a new rule. Every time I blow a whistle, you have to get down on your hands and knees and worship me.
- Blow the whistle several times.
- Ask: Why won't you worship me?
- Say: Of course you know we only worship God.

- Say: But let's see what happened when a king thought that he was more important than God.
- Read "A Burning Faith."
- Say: We will probably never be threatened with losing our lives, but sometimes we will be asked to stand up for our belief in God.
- Make the "Burning Faith" lanterns.

✂

## "BURNING FAITH" LANTERNS

1. Using permanent markers, color the center space of the bottle with red, orange, and yellow flames.
2. Outline the flames with a fine-tip black permanent marker.
3. Cut out the Bible verse strip. Tape around the container as shown.
4. Cut out the figures and tape around the bottom as shown.
5. Bend one half of a chenille stem as shown and insert either end in the holes at the top for a handle.
6. Place a battery-operated tea light inside the container through the hole at the bottom.
7. Ask: Who is the fourth person in the fire?

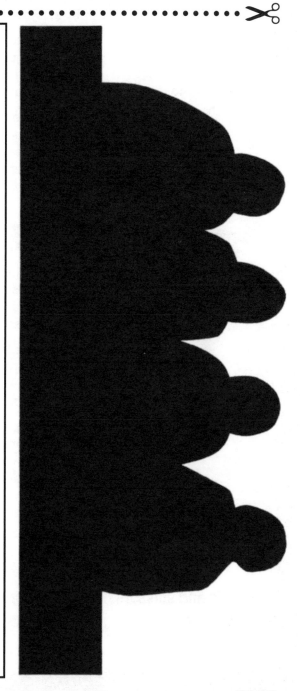

*Worship the Lord your God, and serve only him.*

*Luke 4:8, CEB*

# Daniel's Dilemma

### Bible Story
Daniel 6:1-28

### Bible Verse
I've chosen the way of faithfulness.
   Psalm 119:30, CEB

### Green Message
Choosing to be faithful to God is not always easy.

In a land so far away,
There lived a man who liked to pray.
He prayed to God three times a day.
**Roar. Roar. Roar.**

His name was Daniel, and we know
How he was taken long, long ago,
To a land he did not know.
**Roar. Roar. Roar.**

Daniel was faithful, strong, and true.
He knew just what he had to do.
He served the king and served God too.
**Roar. Roar. Roar.**

Then jealous men dreamed up a plan.
They made a law for all the land.
This law said prayers to God were banned.
**Roar. Roar. Roar.**

But Daniel chose to do what was right.
And in his room within plain sight,
He prayed to God both day and night.
**Roar. Roar. Roar.**

Tho' Daniel was the king's good friend,
All because of those mean men,
He was put into the lion's den.
**Roar. Roar. Roar.**

With lions Daniel spent the night.
The king rushed down at morning's light
To see if Daniel was all right!
**Roar. Roar. Roar.**

"Oh, king, my God took care of me.
I'm safe and sound as you can see.
God's servant I will always be."
**Roar. Roar. Roar.**

## Supplies ...........................................................

**pencils and scissors**
**rubber bands**

**crayons or markers**
**glue sticks**

**lunch-sized paper bags**
**paper plate (circle pattern)**

## Ahead of time:

• Photocopy the parts for the lion puppet.

## Group time:

• Make the lion puppets.
• Ask: What does it mean to be faithful to God? What do you do? What do you NOT do? What happens when you are not faithful?
• Tell the story "Daniel's Dilemma."

OPTION: *The lion parts can be used as patterns and can be cut from construction paper.*

• Have the children make their puppets roar at the designated parts in the story.
• Ask: What law did the king pass that Daniel HAD to disobey? Was it a good law? How did God help Daniel?

## LION PUPPETS

1. Color and cut out the lion's face and tongue.
2. Attach the head to the bottom of a paper bag.
3. Attach the tongue beneath the flap as shown.
4. Trace a paper plate on an opened paper bag.
5. Cut out the circle and make cuts toward the center, leaving three inches uncut in the center.
6. Glue the mane to the back of the paper bag.
7. Cut strips of paper bag to make the whiskers.
8. Gather the bag below the head. Secure with a rubber band.
9. Slip your hand into the bag and make your lion "roar!"

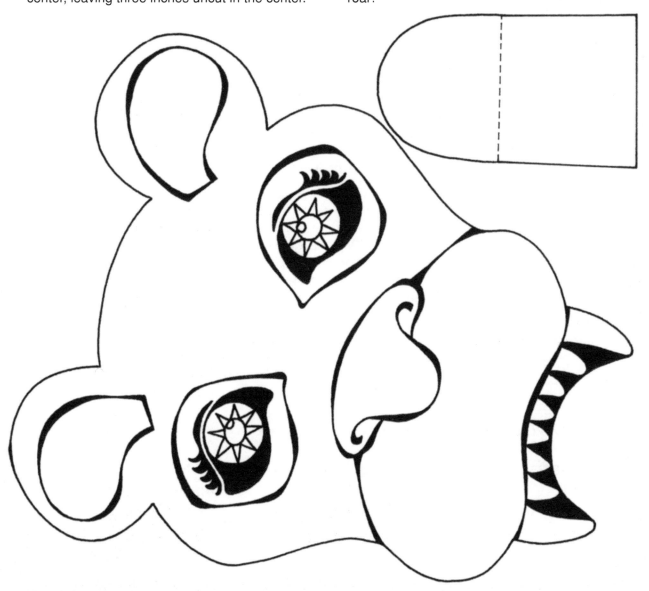

# Courage of a Queen

**Bible Story**
Book of Esther

**Bible Verse**
Be brave and strong and trust the LORD.
Psalm 27:14, CEV

**Green Message**
Sometimes it takes courage to stand up for what is right.

---

**Pronunciation:**
Mordecai (MOR duh-kigh)

The story begins when I was just an ordinary, but beautiful, Jewish girl living in Babylon. The **king** was having a great banquet. It had been going on for weeks and weeks. The **king** decided to show off a bit and ordered the **queen** to drop what she was doing and come to the banquet.

The **queen** was hosting a banquet for the women elsewhere in the palace. She did not want to leave her guests. So the **queen** told the **king** that she was busy. So the **king** set about looking for a new and more obedient **queen**.

My cousin Mordecai, who worked in the palace, told me to try out for the job as **queen**. When the **king** saw me, it was love at first sight. That's how I became the new **queen**. The **king** did not know that I was Jewish. Jewish people were outcasts in the kingdom at this time. No Jewish woman had ever been **queen** before. I decided to tell the **king** later—much later.

One day Mordecai overheard some people talking about a secret plot to have all the Jewish people in the kingdom killed. That would include me. So Mordecai came to me for help. He thought that because the **king** loved me so much, I should beg the **king** to change his mind. I was so scared. But if I didn't do this, who would save our people?

I may have been **queen**, but I needed courage. My actions would save the lives of many people. I knew God would give me the strength I needed. I went to see the **king** unannounced. To my surprise the **king** was glad to see me. I invited him and the chief advisor who had come up with this awful plan to a banquet. The advisor felt very important to be invited to a banquet given by the **queen**.

After they had both eaten, I told the **king** just what his advisor had planned to do to my people—and to me! The **king** was furious. My people were saved, and the advisor lost his job— and his life. But it served him right for being so wicked. Now everyone (except the advisor) is living happily ever after.

## Supplies •••••••••••••••••••••••••••••••••••••

scissors
yarn
craft glue
gift boxes with lids

beads or bottle caps
masking tape
faux gemstones, glitter,
    and metallic trim

utility knife (adult only)
½-inch wooden dowels or
    unsharpened pencils
rubber bands

## Ahead of time:
- Photocopy the directions and the Bible verse for the drums.
- Use a utility knife to cut a hole in one side of the small gift box as shown below. Make the hole large enough for the wooden dowel (or unsharpened pencil) to go through snugly.

## Group time:
- Make the spin drums.
- Ask: What do you think it would be like to be a king or a queen? What kinds of laws would you make? What would be the most important thing you could do?
- Read "Courage of a Queen."

- Have the children listen for the words "king" or "queen." Every time they hear those words, they are to spin their drum.
- Ask: Why did it take courage for Esther to talk to the king? What was more important to her?

✁ ‒ ‒ ‒ ‒ ‒ ‒ ‒ ‒ ‒ ‒ ‒ ‒ ‒ ‒ ‒ ‒ ‒ ‒ ‒ ‒ ‒ ‒ ‒ ‒ ‒ ‒ ✄

### BE-JEWELED SPIN DRUMS

1. Remove the lid from a small gift box.
2. Insert a dowel (or pencil) into the hole and secure with masking tape.
3. Cut a twelve-inch piece of yarn.
4. Lay it across the box as shown so that an equal amount of yarn extends on either side. Tape securely.
5. Trim the yarn so that no more than five inches extends on either side of the box. Tie a wooden bead on each end as shown.

6. Put craft glue around the rim of the box and place the lid on the box. (Make sure the yarn and beads are outside the box.)
7. Hold in place with a rubber band while the glue dries.
8. Cut out the Bible verse to go on the top of the lid. Decorate with faux gemstones, glitter, and metallic trim.

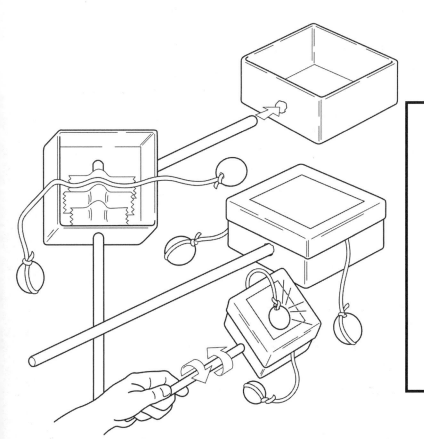

## BE BRAVE AND STRONG AND TRUST THE Lord.

PSALM 27:14, CEV

# Jonah Learns a Lesson

**Bible Story**
Jonah 1:1–3:10

**Bible Verse**
Everyone who loves is born from God and knows God.
　　　1 John:4:7, CEB

**Green Message**
God's love is for everyone.

Once there was a man named Jonah. Jonah obeyed all God's laws. Jonah tried to do everything that God wanted him to.

*I always try to do what's right; to God I'm faithful and true. I try to live the way I should, and do what God wants me to.*

One day God asked Jonah to go to the city of Nineveh. Jonah would tell the people there to straighten up or bad things were going to happen. But Jonah didn't like the people of Nineveh. He wanted bad things to happen to them.

*I always try to do what's right; to God I'm faithful and true. But those people there I do not like, and THAT I will not do.*

So, Jonah hopped on a ship that was going in the opposite direction. He made himself comfortable and took a nap. As he slept, a great storm came up. Jonah knew that God had sent this storm. So he told the sailors to throw him into the water, and then the storm would stop.

*I always try to do what's right; to God I'm faithful and true. You need to throw me in the sea; that's just what you must do.*

At that very moment, God sent a great fish up from the bottom of the sea. The fish opened its mouth and swallowed Jonah whole. For three days Jonah prayed from inside the fish.

*I always try to do what's right; to God I'm faithful and true. Whatever job you have for me, then that's what I will do.*

The fish swam to the surface of the water and spit Jonah out onto the dry land. Jonah went to Nineveh. He told the people what God wanted them to do. The people of Nineveh changed their ways and God forgave them.

*I always try to do what's right; to God I'm faithful and true. I've learned God's family is big enough for me and also for you!*

## Supplies ............................................

| | | |
|---|---|---|
| recycled business-sized envelopes | crayons and markers | stapler, staples |
| glue sticks | scissors | |
| | scrap paper | |

## Ahead of time:

• Photocopy the Jonah Action Figure and great fish for each child.

## Group time:

• Make the action puppet.
• Play a game of musical chairs. In this game no one is eliminated. As you begin removing chairs, the children have to all have a chair in some way. That might mean sitting on one another.

• Ask: What was different about this game? Was it fun to not have anyone eliminated for a change? Did you know God's love is like that?
• Read "Jonah Learns a Lesson." Use the puppets during the story.

## JONAH ACTION FIGURE

1. Color Jonah and the great fish. Cut out.
2. Fold the fish over the envelope. Glue.
3. Cut off both ends of the envelope and remove the area inside the mouth. Use markers to add more ocean below the fish.
4. Fold Jonah on the dotted line.

5. Fold a scrap sheet of paper over and over again until it is 1- by 10-inches. Staple.
6. Tape the paper stick inside Jonah. Staple Jonah's feet through all thicknesses.
7. Thread Jonah through the fish envelope and out of the mouth of the fish as shown.

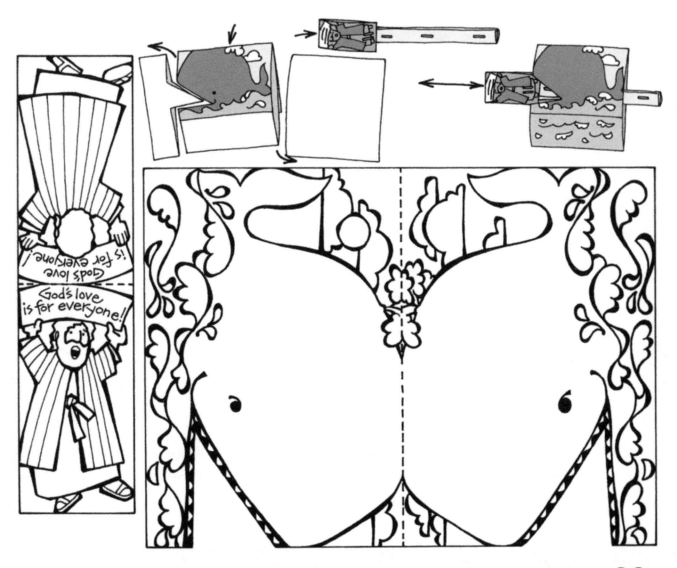

# Micah's Promise

**Bible Story**
Micah 5:2-5

**Bible Verse**
He shall be the one of peace.
  Micah 5:5, NRSV

**Green Message**
God wants people all over the world to live in peace with one another.

Times were not good for God's people. Armies surrounded their little country. The leaders did not trust God to take care of the people. The people felt that God had gone away and left them.

**Micah: Hear me, people, I have a message from God.**

Micah saw what was happening to the poor farmers where he lived. The rich landlords were taking away the land and the houses of the poor. Micah knew that God was not pleased. He knew that God was losing patience with the people.

**Micah: You silly people. You have forgotten just how powerful God really is. Have you forgotten that it was God who led the people out of Egypt? It was God who parted the sea. You need to straighten up, or you'll be sorry.**

Micah knew that when the faith of the people was not strong, then the country would not be strong. Micah knew what a powerful army would do to them. Micah knew that the people had to change their ways or suffer the consequences.

**Micah: You have turned away from God. Because of that, God will not save you from the bad things that are coming.**

Micah knew that God still loved the people very much. There would be a time when God would send someone to save them. This Messiah would be born in Bethlehem and would come from the family of King David.

**Micah: Your Savior is coming! He will change things. He will bring peace to all the world.**

All the bad things that God said would happen happened. The people were captured and taken far away from their homes. They remembered God's promise that one day God would bring them back home.

**Micah: And when the Messiah comes, no person or country will be able to stand against him. He will be the one of peace.**

## Supplies ••••••••••••••••••••••••••••••••••••••••••

sheets of scrap paper
paper clips
glue sticks

yarn
clear tape
water or soda bottles

crayons or markers
scissors

64

## Ahead of time:
- Make a copy of the dove for each child to use as a pattern.
  FAST OPTION: *Photocopy four doves per child.*
- Cut yarn into 24-inch lengths.

## Group time:
- Ask: What would a time look like when the whole world is at peace?
- Read "Micah's Promise."
- Remind the children that Micah was a prophet and that prophets delivered God's messages to the people.
- Ask: What things were happening to God's people that made them look to a time of peace?
- Have the children make the peace mobile.

✂ - - - - - - - - - - - - - - - - - - - - - - - - - - - - - - - - -

### PEACE MOBILE

1. Cut four doves.
2. Fold the wings down.
3. Tape a paper clip to the inside of two of the doves. (The metal loop will show above the wing fold.)
4. Glue a second dove over each dove with a paper clip, so that the clip is between the two doves. Leave the wings free.
5. Fold a sheet of scrap paper in half lengthwise. Open.
6. Tape a 24-inch length of yarn down the center fold, letting an equal amount of yarn extend beyond the paper on either end.
7. Fold the outside edges of the paper to the center fold.
8. Continue to fold until the paper is ½-inch wide. Tape.
9. Repeat with the second sheet of paper, but leave out the yarn.
10. Fold the second strip over the first as shown. Wrap tape around the second strip just below the first strip.
11. Tie the yarn to the metal loop on each dove.
12. Glue the Bible verse onto the bottle.
13. Insert the strip without the doves into the bottle as shown. Spin and watch the doves fly.

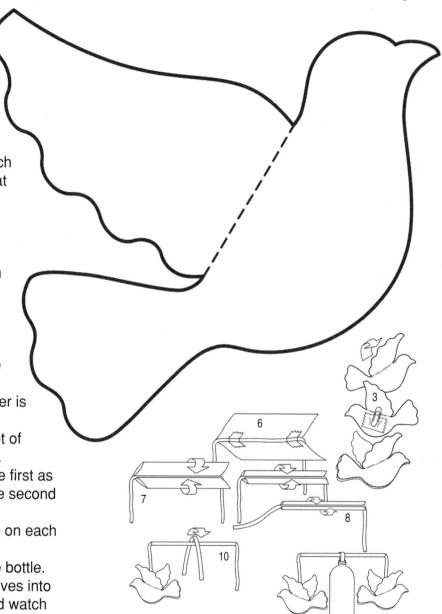

> ## *He shall be the one of peace.*
> *Micah 5:5, NRSV*

# The Peaceful Kingdom

**Bible Story**
Isaiah 11:1-9

**Bible Verse**
Just as water fills the sea, the land will be filled with people who know and honor the LORD.

Isaiah 11:9, CEV

**Green Message**
God sent Jesus to teach us how to live together in peace.

A long time ago there lived a man named Isaiah. He was a prophet of God. We all know that God's prophets deliver God's message to the people. Isaiah had a special message, a message of peace.

Isaiah told the people, "God says that a king is coming. Like a branch that grows from a stump, someone from King David's family will be the king. God will give him understanding and wisdom. His greatest joy will be to obey God."

**Peace is coming! Peace is coming!**

"This king won't judge by appearances or listen to gossip or rumors. He will treat everyone the same. His word will be the law, everywhere in the land.

**Peace is coming! Peace is coming!**

"Leopards will lie down with young goats. Wolves will rest with lambs."

**Peace is coming! Peace is coming!**

"Calves and lions will eat together and be cared for by children."

**Peace is coming! Peace is coming!**

"Cows and bears will share the same pastures. Their young will lie down side by side."

**Peace is coming! Peace is coming!**

"Lions and oxen will both eat straw."

**Peace is coming! Peace is coming!**

"Nothing harmful will happen on the Lord's holy mountain. Just as water fills the sea, the land will be filled with people who know and honor the LORD."

**Peace is coming! Peace is coming!**

## Supplies ...........................................

scissors

crayons or markers

construction paper

cardboard tubes

glue sticks

clear tape

## Ahead of time:
- Photocopy the puppet heads and directions.
- Cut cardboard tubes into four- to six-inch lengths.

## Group time:
- Have the children make the animal puppets for the story.
- Ask the children to hold up the puppets in this grouping: leopard/goat, wolf/lamb, calf/lion, cow/bear, lion/ox. After each pairing, ask: Do these animals get along?

*TIP: Depending on how many cardboard tubes you have, each child can make a whole set of puppets or just a couple.*

- Read "The Peaceful Kingdom." With each pairing, have the children bring that puppet to the front of the group and say the words in bold type.
- Ask: If God's promise of peace means that all these animals would get along, what does that mean for people? Would this be a good thing?

✂

**PEACEFUL KINGDOM PUPPETS**

1. Color each of the animal heads. Cut out.
2. Cover each cardboard tube with construction paper.
3. Glue an animal head to each tube.

lion

ox

wolf

lamb

calf

cow

bear

goat

leopard

# And the Angel Said...

## Bible Story
Luke 1:26-38;
Matthew 1:18-25

## Bible Verse
Nothing is impossible
for God.

Luke 1:37, CEB

## Green Message
Nothing is impossible
for God.

A long time ago in the town of Nazareth, there lived a young girl named Mary and a carpenter named Joseph. They were engaged to be married.

One day as Mary was doing her chores, an **angel** came to her. Mary had never seen an **angel** before. She was scared.

"Don't be afraid, Mary," said the **angel**. "God has sent me to tell you something special. You are going to have a baby. Your baby will be great. He will be a king."

"That's impossible!" Mary exclaimed. "How can this be!"

But the **angel** said, "Nothing is impossible with God."

"Why did God choose me?" Mary asked the **angel**.

"You have found favor with God. Your child will be called the Son of God," said the **angel**.

"I will do whatever God wants me to do," said Mary. The **angel** left. "I must tell Joseph the news," said Mary.

When Joseph heard what the **angel** said, he was worried. "What will people think? What will people say about Mary? What will people say about me? Maybe, we should call off the wedding."

That night as Joseph slept, an **angel** whispered in his ear, "Don't be afraid to take Mary as your wife. The baby is God's Son. You will name him Jesus. He is the one that God promised to send." Then the **angel** left him.

When Joseph woke up from his sleep, he remembered what the **angel** had said to him. He knew then what he must do. He would marry Mary. They would be a family. They would name the baby Jesus. They would be the parents of God's Son.

## Supplies

| | | |
|---|---|---|
| clear plastic deli boxes or lids | three-dimensional paint (gold, silver, metallic) | chenille stems |
| scissors | paper punch | jingle bells |
| tape | metallic ribbon | recycled newspaper |
| | | fine-line marker |

## Ahead of time:

- To save time, cut away the sides of the boxes or lids. Each child needs a flat piece of clear plastic large enough for a six-inch circle.
- Cover the tables with recycled newspaper.
- Cut chenille stems in half.

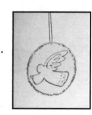

## Group time:

- Ask: How do you or your parents receive messages? Do you get mail? telephone calls? e-mails? text messages? Have you ever received a message from an angel? What do you think an angel sounds like?

- Have each child thread a jingle bell onto half of a chenille stem.
- Read "And the Angel Said..." When the children hear the word *angel*, have them ring their bell.
- Make the angel suncatcher.

✂ - - - - - - - - - - - - - - - - - - - - - - - - - - - - - - - - - - - - - - - - - - - - - - - - - - -

### ANGEL ORNAMENT

1. Cut out the angel pattern, and trace the circle on a piece of clear plastic. Cut out.
2. Place the design on the back side of the plastic and tape lightly to hold it in place.
3. Using metallic three-dimensional paints, outline the angel on the plastic.
4. Set aside the design to dry.
5. When dry, punch a hole at the top and attach a piece of gold or silver ribbon.

# One Special Night

**Bible Story**
Luke 2:1-20

**Bible Verse**
The people who walked in darkness have seen a great light.
Isaiah 9:2, NRSV

**Green Message**
The birth of God's Son Jesus changed the world.

The word went out from the city of Rome;
It's the law—you must go to your ancestor's home.
So Joseph and Mary set off down the road.
The little gray donkey had to bear all the load.
The city was crowded with folks far and wide,
But there wasn't a place for him and his bride.
At last a kind innkeeper gave them a space.
The travelers' stable was the very last place.
And that night in the dark of that stable so warm,
Jesus, God's Son, the Messiah was born.

While up in the hills on that dark, windy night.
The stars were all shining so big and so bright.
But even the fire could not put off the chill
For the sheep and the shepherds who sat on that hill.
When all of a sudden—bright light filled the sky,
And the shepherds heard voices, singing on high.
"We have news that a special child has been born,
In the city below, on this very morn.
We bring you good news of this baby's birth.
He'll bring peace to the world and joy here on earth."

"The child is the Savior, the King of all kings.
And He is the one for whom we now sing.
You'll find him asleep, with hay 'neath his head,
And a manger for livestock now serves as his bed."

Then suddenly there were many more angels to see
Than ever the shepherds thought there ought to be.
They sang songs of praise and peace to the earth.
Their songs celebrated the Holy Child's birth.

"Let us go see this child of whom we've been told,
The child who fulfills all the Scriptures of old."

They found the sweet child as the angels had said,
Asleep in a stable, a manger his bed.
And in that crude stable, so safe and so warm,
God's only Son, the Christ Child was born.

## Supplies

widemouth plastic jars
  (peanut butter)
scissors
white glue and water

black construction paper
small containers
paintbrushes
art tissue (blue, purple)

decorative ribbon
battery-operated
  tea lights
pudding cups

## Ahead of time:

- Photocopy the directions and skyline pattern for each lantern.
- Pre-cut the colored art tissue if time is short.
- OPTION: *Spray paint the lids with black, silver, or gold fusion paint.*

## Group time:

- Ask: Where do kings and queens live? Would you expect to find a king in a stable or a barn? Why not? Why do you think God chose this location for his Son Jesus to be born?
- Read "One Special Night."
- Make the Bethlehem lanterns.

- - - - - - - - - - - - - - - - - - - - - - - - - - - - - - - - - - - - - - - - ✂

### BETHLEHEM LANTERNS

1. Dilute white glue with water so that it is the consistency of milk. Put it in a shallow container.
2. With paintbrushes, paint scraps of dark blue, light blue, and dark purple art tissue onto the jar. Cover completely. Allow to dry.
3. Cut out the Bethlehem skyline.
4. Trace the skyline onto the fold of a piece of black construction paper. Cut out.
5. Cut a ribbon twice as long as the circumference of the top of the container.
6. Paint the top edge of the container with glue and tie the ribbon around the top.
7. Put glue on the back of the skyline and wrap it around the bottle, making sure the bottom edges line up. (HINT: *If the bottom of the container is curved, snip the bottom edge of the skyline in several places and let the pieces overlap slightly for a more secure fit.*)
8. Put glue around the top edge of a pudding cup. Place it inside the jar, with the top of the cup on the bottom of the jar. This will be the candle holder.
9. Place a battery-operated tea light inside the jar on the bottom of the pudding cup.

DO NOT USE A REAL CANDLE.

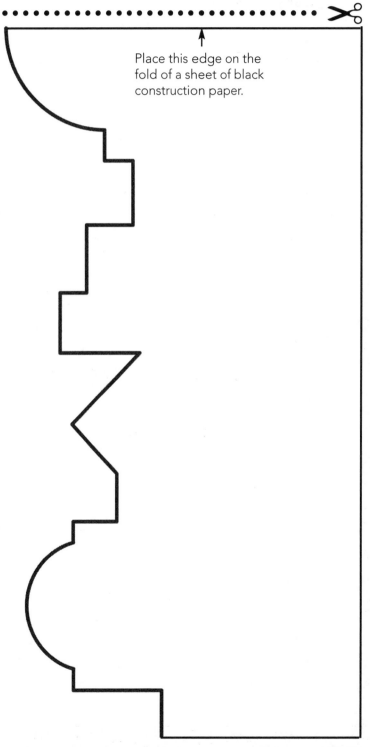

Place this edge on the fold of a sheet of black construction paper.

# Follow That Star!

**Bible Story**
Matthew 2:1-12

**Bible Verse**
Where is the newborn king of the Jews? We've seen his star in the east, and we've come to honor him.
Matthew 2:2, CEB

**Green Message**
Jesus is God's gift to all people everywhere.

Once long ago in the faraway land of Persia, there were men who studied the stars. Every night they would look up into the sky, hoping to learn wonderful things. Then one night it happened—there in the sky was a new star!

"It's a sign," they said to each other. "A new king has been born. Let's find him!" They all agreed that this was what they should do.

These wise men loaded their camels with gifts for the new king and set out following the new star's light. The star led them across deserts and plains, over hills, and through valleys. Soon they came to the land ruled by King Herod.

"Maybe the people in that city can help us. Surely they will know about the birth of a new king." All through the city, the wise men asked everyone they met. "Can you help us find the child who has been born King of the Jews?" But no one knew what they were talking about.

Soon word got to King Herod that some strange looking men were asking about a new king. He was worried. A new king? Maybe he needed to talk with these men. So Herod invited the wise men to the palace. "Who is this new king you are looking for?" he asked them.

"We saw a new star in the sky. That is a sign of the birth of a new king. We are looking for him," said the wise men.

"The ancient Scriptures say that the child will be born in Bethlehem. Go there. Find the child. Then report back to me so I can worship the child, too," said the king.

The wise men found the child in a house in Bethlehem with his mother Mary. They bowed down and worshiped the child, presenting their gifts.

But when the time came for them to go home, they did NOT report back to the king. An angel had warned them to go home by another route. And that is what they did.

## Supplies ·····················································

| | | |
|---|---|---|
| 2 recycled CDs per star | foil wrapping paper | books of constellations |
| white glue | scraps | flashlights |
| scissors | cotton swabs | heavy objects or books |
| pencil | gold/silver craft cord or | to place on glued CDs |
| glue sticks | clear fishing line | (optional) glitter glue |

## Ahead of time:
- Make a copy of the star pattern for each child.
- Cut gold or silver craft cord or clear fishing line into 24-inch lengths.
- Bring in books that show the stars and constellations in the sky.

## Group time:
- Pass around the books and/or pictures of the stars and constellations.
- Ask: How many of you ever spend time looking up at the night sky? What do you see? Which constellations can you find? Did you know that long ago people looked to the sky to tell them when exciting things were going to happen?
- Read "Follow That Star!"
- Ask: What special event did the sky announce one night? What did the men decide to do? What made their visit so special?

- Explain to the children that in Bible times there were two groups of people: the Hebrews and "everyone else." The Hebrew people did not associate with people who were not of their faith. The wise men were part of the "everyone else," but they came in search of the baby as well.
- Make the shiny stars. Hang them in the room. Turn off all the lights and let the children shine their flashlights on them.

• • • • • • • • • • • • • • • • • • • • • • • • • • • • • • • • • • • • • • • • • • • • • • • • • • • • ✂

### STAR ORNAMENTS

1. Tape a length of cord or fishing line securely to the label side of a CD.
2. Using a cotton swab, paint the label side of the second CD with white glue.
3. Place the second CD on top of the first, shiny side up, sandwiching the cord inside. Line up the edges so they are even.

4. Place a book or heavy object on the ornament until the glue sets.
5. Cut out the star pattern.
6. Trace and cut out two stars from scraps of foil gift wrapping paper.
7. Glue a star on both sides of the ornament, covering up the holes in the center.

COOL OPTION: *Decorate both sides of the ornament with glitter glue.*

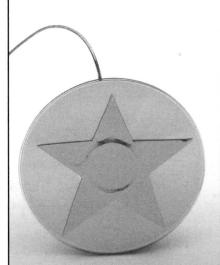

# Jesus and the Elders

**Bible Story**
Luke 2:41-52

**Bible Verse**
Jesus matured in wisdom and years, and in favor with God and with people.
Luke 2:52, CEB

**Green Message**
God plans for us to grow and change as we get older.

Jesus grew up in the small town of Nazareth. Every year in the spring, all the people of Nazareth would leave their fields, their shops, and their homes and go to Jerusalem for the Passover. Thousands of people filled the streets and market-places of the city. It was a very exciting time, especially for a young boy.

This year was special for Jesus. This year he was old enough to go inside the Temple courtyard with Joseph and the other men. No longer did he have to stay outside with his mother and the other "children" of the village.

After seven days, the celebration came to an end. All the people started for home. Everyone was tired but happy. Mary had not seen Jesus, but she thought he was probably with the men who would come later. But when the men caught up with the group, Jesus was not with them.

"We have to go back," said Mary. "Who knows what could have happened to him." They went to all the shopkeepers and asked if they had seen their son. But Jesus was nowhere to be found.

Finally they went to the Temple courtyard. Jesus had spent much time there, talking with the teachers. Perhaps he had lost track of time and had not noticed that everyone had gone.

When they got there, they saw their son sitting at the feet of a group of teachers. He was talking and they were looking at him in amazement. Mary and Joseph rushed up to their son. "We've been looking *everywhere* for you. Do you know how worried we've been?" they asked.

"You should have known I would be here. This is my Father's house." Jesus was an obedient son and he went back to Nazareth with his parents. There he grew in wisdom and in years and in favor with God and people.

## Supplies

| | | |
|---|---|---|
| tape measures, rulers, yardsticks, scale | pencils | |
| yellow copy paper | old file folders | |
| scissors | glue sticks | |
| | masking tape | |

**Ahead of time:**
- Copy the growth chart on yellow paper for each child.
- Cut old file folders into 1 ½- by 18-inch strips.

## Group time:

- Invite the children to use the various measuring tools to measure odd things, such as the circumference of their head, how wide they can spread their arms, etc.
- Ask: As you get older, will these measurements change? What are some other things that will change about you?
- Read "Jesus and the Elders."
- Ask: What was special about this trip to Jerusalem? How did Jesus use this opportunity to learn more about God?
- Make a growth chart to take home and celebrate growing and changing.

### GOLDEN RULER GROWTH CHART

1. Tape four 18-inch cardboard strips end to end.
2. Cut the ruler strips apart.
3. From one end of the long strip, measure up 24 inches. Attach the ruler strips in order on the cardboard strip starting here.
4. Glue or tape the Bible verse and inchworm to the top of the ruler.
5. Tape the ruler to the wall beginning at the floor.
6. Stand with your heels against the wall and let someone mark your height on the ruler.

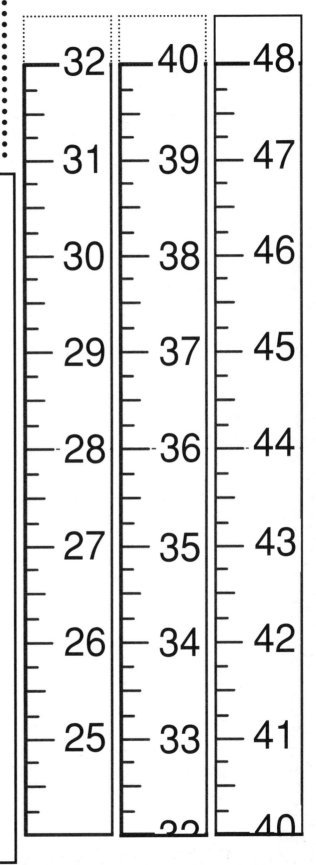

Do to others as you would have them do to you.
Matthew 7:12, NRSV

# Hope for the Hopeless

**Bible Story**
Luke 4:14-30

**Bible Verse**
The Spirit of the Lord is upon me.
Luke 4:18, CEB

**Green Message**
God wants us to help those people who are not as fortunate as we are.

Jesus was now thirty years old. News about him had begun to spread throughout the countryside. He had spent much time away from his hometown of Nazareth, teaching and preaching and healing. He was glad to be home. The people wanted to see Jesus do the same things in their village.

On the sabbath day Jesus came to worship at the synagogue. One of the elders invited Jesus to read the Scripture for the day. Jesus walked to the front and took the scroll from the elder. He unrolled it and began to read:

*The Spirit of the Lord is upon me, because he has chosen me to bring good news to the poor, to set the prisoners free, and to give blind people their sight.*

All eyes were on Jesus as he finished reading. He handed the scroll back to the elder and sat down. The room was so quiet you could hear a pin drop. Then Jesus said, "This Scripture has come true just as you heard it."

The men turned to one another, impressed by the words he had spoken to them. "Isn't this Jesus, son of Joseph, the carpenter? How can he be the one God promised?"

The villagers had all heard the stories about the miracles Jesus had performed. But he had done them somewhere else. Since he had been home, he had not done one miraculous thing. "Are other cities and towns and people more deserving of God's promise?" they wondered.

This made them angry. In fact, some of the men became so angry that they ran Jesus out of town. Jesus was sad that even his friends and neighbors did not accept who he was.

## Supplies

- brown paper grocery bags or parcel paper
- scissors
- string, yarn, or jute
- permanent felt-tip markers or crayons
- container of water
- towels
- recycled newspaper
- iron (adults only)

## Ahead of time:

- Photocopy the directions for the scrolls.
- Set up an "ironing center" that is away from the normal activity area.
- Cover the area under the container of water with recycled newspaper.
- Cut the grocery bags or parcel paper into 9- by 12-inch rectangles.

## Group time:

- Ask: What are some of the things that you know from hearing stories about Jesus? Do you know some things that Jesus taught people to do? How do you know these things? What special book can you read to learn about Jesus?
- Say: The part of the Bible we call the "Old Testament" was around when Jesus was preaching and teaching.

- Point out that people knew about the promise of a coming Messiah.
- Read "Hope for the Hopeless."
- Ask: Who are the people in our world who are hopeless? Who needs Jesus' message?
- Make the Good News scrolls.

✂

### GOOD NEWS SCROLLS

1. Use crayon or permanent felt-tip markers to write: "Jesus brings good news to everyone" in the center of a 9- by 12-inch rectangle of brown paper.
2. Add illustrations or a border.

3. Dip the paper into water. Then squeeze the water out, and lay the paper flat on a towel.
4. With adult assistance, "iron" the scroll dry.
5. Roll up the scroll and tie it with string, yarn, or jute.

# Follow Me

**Bible Story**
Matthew 4:18-22;
Mark 3:13-19

**Bible Verse**
"Come, follow me,"
he said, "and I'll show
you how to fish for
people."
　　Matthew 4:19, CEB

**Green Message**
Jesus calls us to be
disciples and follow
his teachings.

The fishing village stretched along the shore of Lake Galilee. Nets were hung on racks near the beached boats as men and women went about doing their jobs. The Sea of Galilee provided enough fish for the people who lived here.

Andrew and Simon were brothers. They were also fishermen. Their father had been a fisherman, like his father before him. They had a fishing business on Lake Galilee. Every morning they would sort the fish to sell in the village. Simon and Andrew had just come in from a long night of fishing.

A man stood nearby and watched the two brothers for awhile. The man was Jesus. He was looking for people to help him spread the good news of the kingdom of God. He walked up to the brothers. "Simon! Andrew! Come with me and we will catch people for the kingdom of God instead of fish for the market."

The two fishermen pulled their boat up on the shore, stored their nets in the boat, and followed Jesus. Jesus now had two helpers. As they walked a little farther down the beach, they came upon Zebedee's sons James and John. They were sitting in their boat mending their nets. Jesus walked up to them.

"James, John, follow me, and I will teach you to fish for people instead of fish." Just as Simon and Andrew had done, James and John left their nets and their father, and followed Jesus. Now Jesus had four helpers.

One by one Jesus called people to help him. Soon Jesus had twelve helpers: Simon, Andrew, James, John, Philip, Bartholomew; Matthew, Thomas, James the son of Alphaeus, Thaddaeus, Simon the Cananaean, and Judas. Everywhere Jesus went, they went with him. They listened to what Jesus had to say. They helped Jesus spread the good news of God's kingdom. They were called the twelve apostles.

## Supplies ......................................................

　　　net produce bags
　　　　　(onions, peppers)
　　　colored duct tape
　　　white athletic shoelaces

　　scissors
　　fine-point felt-tip markers
　　paper punch

## Ahead of time:

- Photocopy the net bottle holder directions for each child.
- Cut the top brad away from the net bag. Stay as close to the brad as possible.

## Group time:

- Ask: How many of you have ever been fishing? What kind of equipment do you use? Did you know that fishing has not changed very much since Bible times?
- Read "Follow "Me."

- Ask: What did Jesus ask the four fishermen to do? What would they be catching instead of fish?
- Make net bottle carriers that will remind the children that they can be disciples of Jesus, too.

## NET BOTTLE HOLDER

1. Cut a piece of colored duct tape about twenty-four inches long. Place it sticky side up on the table.
2. Place the top edge of the net bag onto the duct tape, leaving about one inch of duct tape above it. (Ask a friend to help you.)
3. Continue rolling the bag onto the duct tape until you go all the way around.
4. Fold the duct tape over the net bag, aligning the edges. (It doesn't have to be totally smooth.)

5. Punch holes around the duct tape as shown here about ½ inch from the edge. Go all the way around.
6. Decorate a white shoestring, using fine-point felt-tip markers.
7. Thread the shoestring through the holes.
8. Place a water bottle inside the net bag and pull the shoestring until the top gathers. Tie the shoestring onto a belt loop or backpack to carry your water.

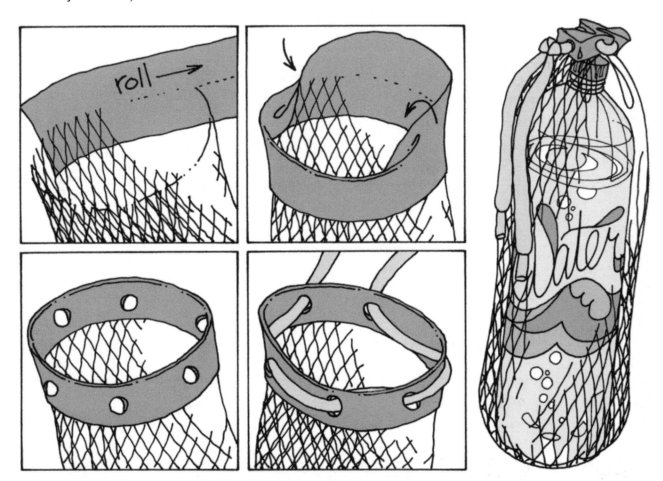

# A Boy's Lunch

**Bible Story**
John 6:1-14

**Bible Verse**
Don't forget to do good and to share what you have.
Hebrews 13:16, CEB

**Green Message**
God multiplies even our smallest gifts into something wonderful.

Everywhere that Jesus went, people followed. They wanted to hear what he had to say. They wanted to see what he would do. One day Jesus was on a hillside talking to his disciples. He looked up and saw a large crowd of people coming toward him.

"It is getting late. These people will need food," said Jesus.

"Feed them? There are thousands of people here. We do not have enough money to feed so many people. It would take more than we make in a year!" said Philip.

Jesus knew that they could not afford to feed so many people. He already knew what he was going to do.

Andrew came up to Jesus. "There is a boy here who is willing to share what he brought to eat. But he has only five loaves of barley bread and two fish. That won't go very far."

"Have the people sit down on the ground," Jesus said. He took the lunch that the boy had brought. Jesus held the bread up and gave thanks for it. He broke it into pieces and handed the bread to the disciples. "Pass this out. Then when everyone has eaten all they care to eat, collect the leftovers so that nothing goes to waste."

The disciples looked at one another. *Leftovers!* they thought to themselves. *There is hardly enough for a young boy, much less a crowd of thousands.* But they did as Jesus asked.

When they brought the leftovers to Jesus, there were twelve full baskets. The people were amazed at what they had seen. To them, this was proof that Jesus was the one whom God had promised them.

*Supplies* ...............................................................

scissors
recycled magazines

stapler, staples
oyster crackers

fish-shaped crackers
bowls, scoops

## Ahead of time:

- Photocopy the directions for the basket.
- Set out bowls of oyster crackers and fish-shaped crackers. Provide a scoop for each bowl.

## Group time:

- Ask: What was the last trip you took with your family? When you got hungry, what did you do? Could you do that in Bible times? Why not?
- Read "A Boy's Lunch."

- Ask: Was the boy's lunch really enough to feed a crowd of 5000 people? How did this happen? How did the people feel when they saw it?
- Make the baskets and scoop crackers into them. If you have time, make extras to share.

✂

### THE BOY'S BASKET

a. Begin with a colorful page from a recycled magazine (about 7 ¾ by 10 ½ inches).
b. Fold the page in half lengthwise.
c. Fold the page in half again.
d. Open the paper out flat.
e. Fold in half the other direction. Then fold in half again.
f. Open the paper. (It will have 16 rectangles.)
g. Bring the top and bottom flaps into the center fold. Crease.
h. Fold corner A until it touches line B as shown. Repeat on each corner.
i. Fold up the two flaps so that the corners are tucked inside.

j. Hold the centers of the two folded flaps. Pull them apart to open the basket.
k. Pinch each corner from the top to the bottom to give the basket a square shape.
l. Use a second magazine page for the handle. Fold in half lengthwise.
m. Open flat. Fold the outside edges to the center fold. Crease.
n. Fold the outside edges into the center. Repeat. Staple several times along the loose edge.
o. Staple to the sides of the box as shown.
p. Add fish-shaped crackers and oyster crackers to be the boy's bread and fish.

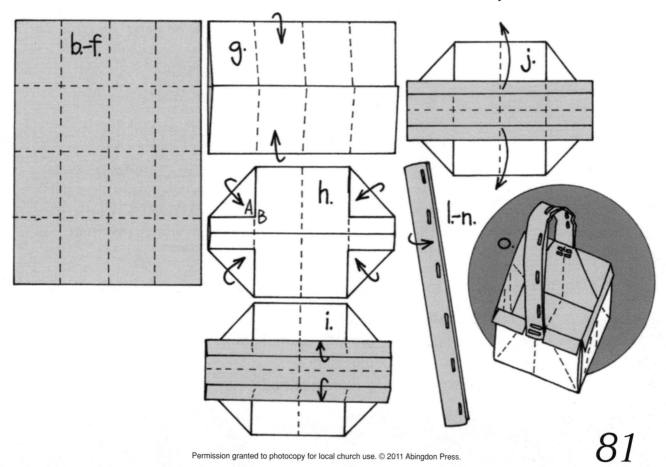

# Be Still!

**Bible Story**
Luke 8:22-25

**Bible Verse**
He commands even the winds and the water, and they obey him!
Luke 8:25, CEB

**Green Message**
God is in charge of everything.

Jesus and his friends had been with a crowd of people all day long. They were very tired. "People, people, people! I've never seen so many people," said Peter impatiently.

"They are hungry to know more about God and how God wants them to live. I can't turn them away," said Jesus.

"But can't we get away for just a little while?" said Andrew.

"We do need a rest. Let's go to the other side of the lake. We can take your boat," said Jesus.

So Jesus and his friends got into the boat. They rowed to the center of the lake. Jesus went to the back of the boat and lay down on cushions and was soon fast asleep.

"Finally, a chance to relax," said Peter. *(Begin waves.)*

"Don't get too comfortable," said Andrew. "Look at those storm clouds over there. They are coming fast." *(faster)*

"Maybe we should head for shore," said Peter, anxiously.

Storms on the lake came up quickly. Soon the wind began to blow. Waves crashed over the sides and the boat began to fill with water. The disciples hung on for dear life, but Jesus continued to sleep in the back of the boat. *(faster)*

"How can he sleep in this storm?" yelled Peter over the wind. "If this keeps up, we're going to sink." *(faster)*

"We need help!" screamed Andrew. "Wake Jesus up!"

Peter shakes Jesus, "Wake up. We're all going to die!"

"Why are you so afraid?" asked Jesus, "Don't you have faith in God?" *(even faster and louder)*

"We have faith, but the boat is sinking!" shouted Peter.

Jesus stood up and spoke to the wind and water, "Be still." The wind stopped blowing; the waves became still. *(Stop.)*

The disciples looked at one another, "Who is this man that even the wind and water obey him?"

## Supplies

| | | |
|---|---|---|
| aluminum pie pans with plastic lids | electrical tape | blue food coloring |
| scissors | crayons or markers | water |
| gravel or birdseed | glue sticks | |
| | 2-liter soda bottle | |

## Ahead of time:

- Make a copy of the Ocean Drum directions and Bible verse insert.
- Make a wave bottle by filling a 2-liter soda bottle with water. Put a few drops of blue food coloring inside the bottle. Close the cap tightly.

## Group time:

- Hold the soda bottle with the water on its side. Rock it back and forth causing a wave-like motion of the water.
- Ask: What does this remind you of? Have you ever been on the water? When the water gets rough, are you afraid? Why?
- Make ocean drums.
- Let the children practice using them to create the sound of the ocean.
- Read "Be Still!" Have the children use their drums to make the sound of the storm, getting louder and then stopping.
- Ask: Why were the disciples afraid? What did Jesus do? Why were they amazed?

✂

## OCEAN DRUM

1. Color the picture of the boat and the water. Cut out.
2. Glue the picture to the top of the plastic lid, using a glue stick. Allow a few minutes for the glue to dry.
3. Put ¼ cup of gravel or birdseed inside the pie tin.
4. Place the lid on the pie pan and tape around the edge with electrical tape. This prevents the lid from coming off and the gravel or birdseed spilling on the floor.
5. Practice swirling the pie tin to make the sound of the ocean.

*He commands even the winds and the water, and they obey him!*

*Luke 8:25, CEB*

# Blind Bartimaeus

**Bible Story**
Mark 10:46-52

**Bible Verse**
Hear my prayer, O LORD.
Psalm 102:1, NRSV

**Green Message**
We can ask for God's help for ourselves and for others.

**Pronunciation:**
Bartimaeus
(bahr-tuh-MEE-uhs)

Once there was a man named Bartimaeus. Bartimaeus was blind. All day long he would sit by the city gates, begging for money. He could not see the people as they passed by, but he could hear them. As they passed, he would call out to them:

**I may be blind and cannot see, but I can hear you walk by me. A loaf of bread; a hunk of meat; if I don't beg, then I can't eat.**

The people thought Bartimaeus was noisy. He was annoying. People gave him money just so he would be quiet.

One day Jesus and his friends were leaving the city of Jericho. As they walked past the city gates, Bartimaeus called out:

**I may be blind and cannot see, but I can hear you walk by me. A loaf of bread; a hunk of meat; if I don't beg, then I can't eat.**

The people who were with Jesus tried to hush the man. "Jesus is a busy man," said one of the group. "He doesn't have time for you. Be quiet. Let him go on his way." But Bartimaeus would not be quiet. He would not let Jesus go on his way:

**I may be blind and cannot see, but I can hear you walk by me. A loaf of bread; a hunk of meat; if I don't beg, then I can't eat.**

Jesus stopped. "Who is that? What does he want?"

"It is only Bartimaeus," said one of the crowd members. "Every day he sits beside the gate and calls out to everyone who passes by, begging for money."

"Bartimaeus," said Jesus. "What do you want me to do for you?" Bartimaeus could hardly believe his ears. He had heard about Jesus and what Jesus could do. Here was his chance.

"Teacher," said Bartimaeus. "I want to see again."

"Then, go. Your faith has made you well," said Jesus. At once Bartimaeus could see and he began to follow Jesus.

## Supplies ........................................................

15-ounce soup cans
medium-sized balloons
spray paint designed
    for plastic (optional)

blindfold
variety of items
    to identify blindfolded
crayons or markers

craft glue or tape
scissors
sharp scissors
    (adult only)

## Ahead of time:

• Photocopy the directions and patterns for the Prayer Drum for each child.

## Group time:

1. Put a variety of items on the floor in the center of the room. One at a time assign each child to find a particular item while they are blindfolded.
2. Ask: Was it hard to find the item? Why?
3. Say: Most people depend on their eyes to live in our world today. Those people who have lost their vision have to discover other ways to function. In Bible times it was not that easy.
4. Read "Blind Bartimaeus."
5. Ask: How did Bartimaeus support himself? Why did he especially want to meet Jesus? Why did he want to be healed? Is it OK to ask for the help of our friends? of God?
6. Remind the children that we can ask God's help for ourselves and for others.
7. Make a prayer drum.

- - - - - - - - - - - - - - - - - - - - - - - - - - - - - - - - - - - - - - - - - - - ✂

### THE PRAYER DRUM

1. Cut out the can wrap with the prayer guide on it. Color.
2. Attach the can wrap to the can. (COOL OPTION: *Use spray paint for plastic to paint the cans in bright primary colors before attaching the wrap. The paint dries quickly.*)
3. Cut the end from a medium-sized balloon.
4. Stretch the balloon over the open end of the can.
5. Pluck the drum as shown as you include each of the sections of your prayer.
6. Use this guide to help you with your prayers each night.

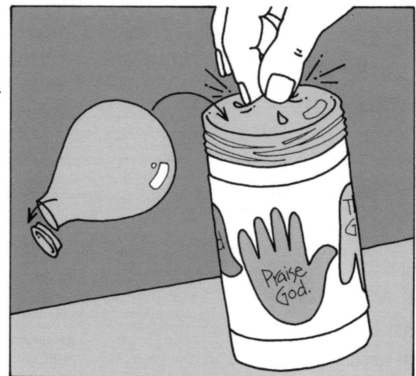

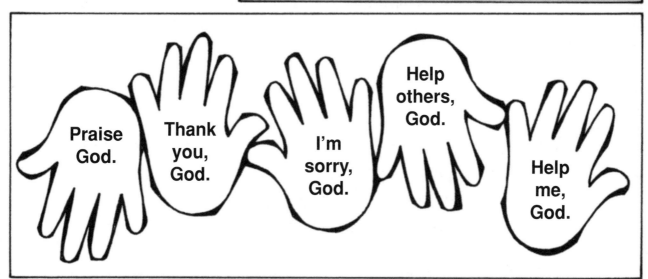

Praise God.

Thank you, God.

I'm sorry, God.

Help others, God.

Help me, God.

# Martha and Mary

**Bible Story**
Luke 10:38-42

**Bible Verse**
Teach me to follow you.
Psalm 86:11, CEV

**Green Message**
God wants us to set priorities in our lives.

As Jesus traveled from place to place, he would often stay with friends. One family that he spent time with was a brother and two sisters—Lazarus, Martha, and Mary.

"Busy, busy, busy. So much to do; so little time," said Martha.

"Why are you so busy, Martha?" asked her sister Mary.

"Jesus is coming! He is bringing his friends!" said Martha.

"How wonderful! I love it when he comes to visit. I love to hear his stories. We have so much to catch up on," said Mary.

"There will be no time for that, Mary. You need to help me get everything ready," said Martha.

Martha swept the dirt floor with her straw broom. She went to the village well to get water. Then she went to the market to get fresh pomegranates. "Mary, come quickly. We need firewood for the oven. I must bake more bread," said Martha.

"Martha, Jesus and his friends will not eat all the bread we have. You don't need to spend so much time cooking and cleaning. Jesus doesn't care about that. He cares about you," said Mary.

"But there's *so much to do* and *so little time,*" said Martha. "Jesus will be here soon. Don't just sit there. *Do something!*"

When Jesus and his friends arrived, Martha was still hurrying about. But Mary came to where Jesus was sitting. She sat down and listened to the things he had to say.

"Jesus! Tell Mary to get up and help me," said Martha angrily. "She has left me to do all the work."

"Martha, you are so worried about things that aren't really important. We will always need food, but I will not always be here. Choose me. That is important right now, today," said Jesus.

## Supplies ...........................................................

shirt
loaf of bread
scissors

colorful fabric
stiff cardboard
masking tape

yardstick

## Ahead of time:
- Make a copy of the directions for weaving the belt.
- Cut pieces of stiff cardboard 4-inches wide and 15-inches long.

## Group time:
- Have the children determine where the shirt was made and who made the loaf of bread.
- Ask: In Bible times if you outgrew your clothing, could you go to the store and buy more? If you wanted a loaf of bread, how did you get it?
- Point out to the children that food and clothing in Bible times had to be made by the women of the household. It took a lot of time.
- Read "Martha and Mary."
- Ask: Why was Martha upset with her sister? Why wasn't Mary helping her sister? What did Jesus say to them?
- Have the children weave a belt to appreciate the work that had to be done.

## WOVEN BELT

a. Cut five notches as shown on both ends of a cardboard strip.

b. Cut or tear strips of fabric about one inch wide. Tie them together to form five strips that are at least 36 inches long.

c. Slip the end of each fabric strip into the notches as shown, leaving a 12-inch tail. Use masking tape to secure the ends on the back of the cardboard loom.

d. Cut or tear additional strips of fabric about one inch wide. Use a wide variety of colors.

e. Begin weaving a strip over and under the strips on the loom. Pull the strip all the way through before starting the next row.

TIP: *Leave a tail at the beginning and weave it back on itself to keep it from coming undone.*

f. When you reach the opposite side, turn and go back again. Weave under and over in the opposite way to the row above.

g. As you run out of fabric, tie another piece onto the front end and continue.

h. When you have finished the last row, weave the end of your fabric back on itself so that it doesn't come undone.

i. Slip the five long strips out of the notches and tie the tails together as shown. Use your new weaving as a colorful belt.

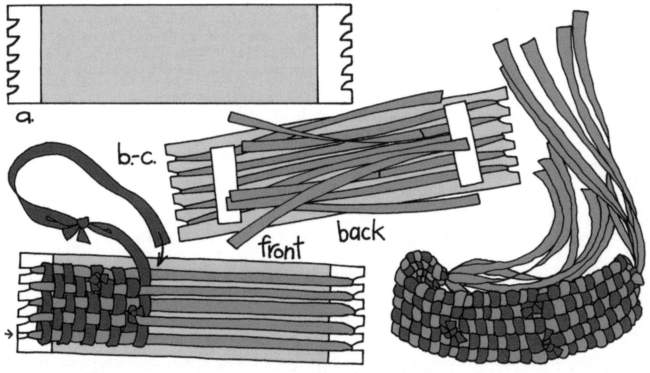

a.

b.-c.

front

back

# Four Friends

## Bible Story
Mark 2:1-12

## Bible Verse
You should praise the LORD for his love and for the wonderful things he does for all of us.
Psalm 107:21, CEV

## Green Message
Friends help one another.

**Friends:** Jesus, Jesus, we have heard
that you can heal with a single word.
It wouldn't take so very much,
for you to use your healing touch. **

One day Jesus was visiting some friends. The news soon spread that he was in town. People came from nearby villages and towns in order to see him and hear him. Some came because they wanted him to heal them. In the crowd there were some Pharisees and teachers of the Law who wanted to learn more about Jesus, too. They were worried about what he taught. **

The small house where Jesus was staying soon became so crowded that there was not room for one more person. In the town there was a man who could not walk. The doctors had not been able to make him well. His friends wondered if maybe Jesus could help him. So the men put their friend on a pallet and carried him to where Jesus was teaching. **

When they got to the house, there were so many people that they could not get inside at all. How could Jesus see there friend now? Suddenly, one of the men had an idea. The men carried their friend up to the roof of the house. Then one by one, they removed the tiles until there was a hole in the roof–a hole just big enough for their friend's bed. **

The men tied ropes to the pallet and lowered their friend into the room, in front of Jesus. Jesus looked at the man on the bed. Then he looked up at the friends on the roof. These men truly believed that Jesus could heal their friend. "Friend," said Jesus, "your sins are forgiven." **

The Pharisees and teachers of the Law gasped. How could Jesus say such a thing. Only God could forgive sins.

"Would it easier for me to say 'stand up and walk?' Either way you will know that I speak with the power of God," said Jesus. Then he looked at the man, "Take up your bed and walk." And the man did. **

## Supplies .......................................

| | | |
|---|---|---|
| scissors | cardboard tubes | plastic drinking |
| scrap cardboard | crayons or markers | straws |
| old file folders | glue sticks | |

## Ahead of time:
- Photocopy "The Carrying Game," one for each pair of children.
- Cut paper towel rolls into three-inch sections.

## Group time:
- Ask: What do you and your friends do together? Do you ever help one another? How?
- Read "Four Friends," with the children repeating the refrain when they see **.
- Ask: How did the four friends help their friend?
- Ask: What did Jesus do when he saw their friendship and their faith?
- Have the children make the game and be the men carrying their friend to see Jesus.

• • • • • • • • • • • • • • • • • • • • • • • • • • • • • • • • • • • • • • • • • • • • • • • • • ✂

### THE CARRYING GAME
1. Color and cut out the man on the mat.
2. Glue the picture on an old file folder. Trim.
3. Glue two small cardboard tubes to the bottom of a cardboard rectangle to make a pallet as shown.
4. Insert a drinking straw in each tube.
5. Place the man on the mat on the pallet.

### How to Play
Invite a friend to play with you, just as the man invited friends to help him. One person will stand on one side of the cardboard pallet, holding one end of the first straw. The other person will stand on the opposite side of the pallet, holding one end of the second straw. Together, carry the man from one side of the room to the other without dropping him.

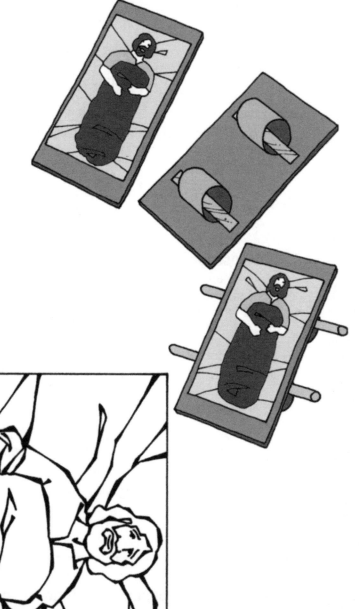

# Who Is My Neighbor?

**Bible Story**
Luke 10:25-37

**Bible Verse**
Love your neighbor as you love yourself.
     Matthew 19:19, CEB

**Green Message**
Jesus teaches us to love our neighbors—both near and far away.

Once there was a man traveling on his way from Jerusalem to Jericho. The road was very dangerous. Bandits were known to hide along the road and attack unsuspecting travelers.

Sure enough, bandits were waiting in the rocks and jumped the man. They beat him up, and took his clothes and his money. Then the bandits left him there beside the road to die.

As it happened a priest was traveling on this same road. He saw the man lying beside the road. "I would like to stop to help the man, but he looks like he might be dead or will be dead soon. If I touch a dead person, I will become unclean. Then I will be unable to do my job. So, I think I'll just walk on the other side of the road and pretend that I don't even see him."

A short time later another man came down the road. He was a Levite, a servant of the Temple. He was carrying money in a sack. He saw the man lying beside the road. "I would like to stop to help the man. He looks like he is hurt. But he could be a bandit, only pretending to be hurt. In that case, stopping would not be smart. So, I think I'll just walk on the other side of the road and pretend that I don't even see him."

Later another man was traveling down the road. He was a Samaritan, someone the traveler would not expect to stop and help him. The Samaritan saw the injured man. He did not worry about becoming unclean. He did not worry about being robbed. And he did not pass by on the other side of the road.

The Samaritan stopped. He treated the man's wounds. Then he put the man on his very own donkey and took him to a nearby inn to care for him. When the Samaritan left, he gave the innkeeper additional money to care for the man.

Of the three, which one was the good neighbor?

## Supplies ...................................................

**food boxes (small popcorn, rice, cracker)**
**index card (pattern)**

**crayons or markers**
**scissors**
**glue sticks**

**wooden craft sticks**
**pencils**
**utility knife (adult only)**

## Ahead of time:

- Photocopy the directions and cut-outs for each child.
- Use an index card as a pattern to cut an opening in the front of each box, and then cut a slit about one inch wide across the top.

## Group time:

- Say: Jesus often told stories to help people know what God wanted them to do. Today we are going to hear a story that talks about neighbors.
- Have the children make the mini-theater and prepare the puppet figures for the presentation.

- Read "Who Is My Neighbor?" As you tell the story, have the children present it using their puppets and mini-theaters.
- Ask: Who did Jesus say was our neighbor? What are neighbors called to do?

1. Color and cut out the background and figures.
2. Glue the background to the inside back of the box, centering it on the opening.
3. Tape the roadside and injured man to the front edge of the box, just below the opening.
4. Glue each figure to a wooden craft stick.
5. Insert the story figures from the top as shown.

**MINI PUPPET THEATER**

91

# The Loving Father

**Bible Story**
Luke 15:11-32

**Bible Verse**
For you, O Lord, are good and forgiving.
    Psalm 86:5, NRSV

**Green Message**
God's love is always there for us.

Jesus often told stories to help people know what God was like. One of the stories was about a father who had two sons. One son was hardworking and dependable; the other son was impatient and reckless.

One day the younger son came to his father and said, "Father, I know that one day your land and fortune will be part mine, but I don't want to wait. I want it now!" So his father divided the family wealth between his two sons. The younger son set off to see the world.

At first life was very exciting for the younger son. People wanted to be around him because he had money to spend. But when the money ran out, so did the friends. The younger son was broke and had to go to work for a farmer who raised pigs. The younger son didn't like pigs very much. They were dirty. They were smelly. But he didn't have a choice. Besides, he could eat some of the food that was thrown to the pigs.

One day as the younger son was watching the pigs, he thought to himself, *Even the servants in my father's household live better than this. I'm going home.* And he did.

As the young man walked down the road toward his father's house, his father ran to greet him. "You've come home! I always hoped you would. Let's have a party!"

But the older brother was not as happy to see his brother. "My brother wasted all your money. Now he's back, broke and begging for help. Why are you being so nice to him? You haven't *ever* given *me* a party!"

"Son, everything I own is yours, and I love you greatly. I'm celebrating because the son I thought was lost has come back home."

What does this say to us about God?

## Supplies ................................................

crayons or markers
white scrap paper
    (blank on one side)
scraps of wrapping paper

faux gemstones
    or buttons
snack mix, cookies
    or trail mix

scissors
craft glue
pencils
potato chip cans

## Ahead of time:
- Photocopy the directions and patterns for each child.
- Let children who have fathers and stepfathers make more than one of these.

## Group time:
- Ask: How did Jesus address God whenever he prayed? Do we refer to God sometimes as our "Father" as well?
- Say: Jesus often used stories to help people know more what God was like. In today's story, the people see God as a forgiving father.
- Read "The Loving Father."
- Ask: Did the younger son really deserve to be treated so well? What was Jesus trying to tell people about God in this story?
- Make a gift for a special "father."

✂

## A GIFT FOR FATHERS

1. Cut white scrap paper so that it will wrap around the can completely. This will be the shirt base.
2. Decorate the blank side of the scrap paper.
3. Glue the shirt base around the can.
4. Use the pattern to trace and cut out a tie from a piece of colorful wrapping paper.
5. Put glue on the "knot" of the tie, and attach the tie to the can as shown here.
6. Attach a button or faux gemstone to the tie as a tie tac.
7. Use the pattern to trace and cut a collar from white scrap paper.
8. Glue the collar to the can, centering it on the knot of the tie as shown.
9. Fill the can with snack mix, trail mix, or a favorite type of cookies.
10. Give this gift to your father or another special man in your life.

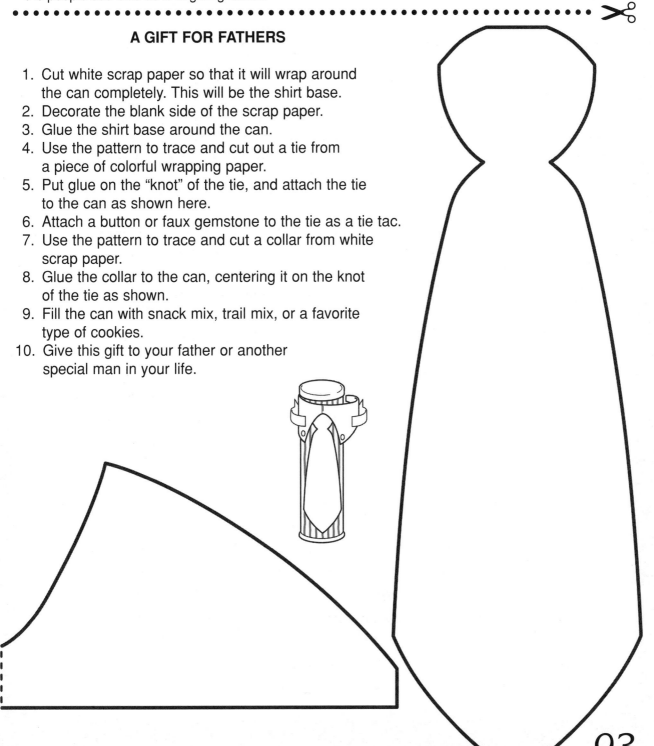

93

# Two Builders

**Bible Story**
Matthew 7:24-28

**Bible Verse**
The LORD is my rock.
Psalm 18:2, NRSV

**Green Message**
Following Jesus' teachings builds a strong faith foundation for our lives.

Jesus told a story about two builders. Both wanted to build a house for their family. Both wanted to build their house of clay bricks. Both wanted a house with a good roof that would protect those who lived inside. Both wanted to build a good house. Both wanted to build a strong house.

The first builder said to himself, "There are so many places where I can build a house. I might as well choose somewhere easy. A dry stream bed would be nice. It is flat and the earth is softer and easier to dig. That is where I will build my house."

The second builder said to himself, "Location, location, location. That's the most important thing. A stream bed would be easy to build on. But what will happen when the rains come? I think I will look for higher land and a place where there are many rocks so I can build a strong foundation. That's where I will build my house."

So the two builders set off to build their houses. Soon both houses were finished. Then the rainy season came...

"Wait," said the first builder. "What is happening to my house? The stream bed has become a river. It is washing away the foundation of my house."

The second builder stood inside his house. The rains came and pounded on the roof. But the little house stood strong.

"My house is safe and dry," said the second builder. "All the work I did is now paying off. My family is safe and dry inside."

God's Word is like the foundation of a house. If we follow God's laws, then our faith foundation will be strong. No rain, no storm will ever be able to shake us.

## Supplies

| | | |
|---|---|---|
| cardboard | small pebbles | utility knife (adult only) |
| crayons or markers | baking pan | 8-ounce milk/juice |
| scissors | sand | cartons |
| white glue | pitcher of water | |
| glue sticks | scrap paper (optional) | |

## Ahead of time:

- Photocopy the house on the rock.
- Remove the tops of the cartons with a utility knife. (Adult only.)
- Cut cardboard into eight-inch squares.

## Group time:

- Place a mound of sand in the center of a baking pan. Pour water over it. Then put a mound of pebbles on the pan. Pour water over it.
- Ask: What is the difference between the two? Which one would you rather build a house on?

*TIP: The reproducible has a roof, a front, a back, and one side. Make extra copies so each house will have two sides, or let the children cover the blank side with scrap paper.*

- Read "Two Builders."
- Tell the children that Jesus was telling this story to help people understand why it was important follow God's teachings in their lives.
- Make the houses.

- - - - - - - - - - - - - - - - - - - - - - - - - - - - - - - - ✂

### THE HOUSE ON THE ROCK

1. Trace the bottom of the carton onto the center of the cardboard.
2. Cover the area thickly with white glue.
3. Place a small layer of pebbles on the glue. Set aside to dry.
4. Color the sections of the house. Cut out.
5. Glue the roof on the bottom of the carton. Fold the back section down and glue. Add the front and side sections.
6. Set the house on the stone foundation.

set house on foundation

fold on dotted line, cut on solid lines

roof + back... copy one

sides ...copy two

front... copy one

95

# Don't Worry!

**Bible Story**
Matthew 6:25-34

**Bible Verse**
Don't worry about
your life.
  Matthew 6:25, CEB

**Green Message**
God cares about us
and provides what
we need.

Jesus went about the countryside teaching people what God was like. Jesus wanted the people to know that they could trust God to care for them.

**Worry Warts: Worry, worry, worry. Whatever shall we do?**

Jesus told the people, "Don't worry so much. Life is more than just food or drink. Look at the birds. Birds don't plant food or harvest food and store it in barns. And still God feeds them. Aren't you more important to God than birds?"

**Worry Warts: Worry, worry, worry. Whatever shall we do?**

Jesus said, "What does all that worry do for you? Does it make you feel better? Does it keep you from becoming ill or getting hurt? Will it add one more hour to your life?"

**Worry Warts: Worry, worry, worry. Whatever shall we do?**

Jesus said to them, "You worry about what clothing to wear. Will you be warm enough? Will your clothing be the right thing to wear? Look around you. Look at the flowers in the field. Flowers don't worry about what they will wear. Flowers don't spin the wool or weave it into cloth. And no king or queen has ever worn a garment more beautiful than the lily growing there. If God provides such clothes for the flowers and grasses, are you not more important than that?"

**Worry Warts: Worry, worry, worry. Whatever shall we do?**

Jesus said to them, "Don't you have any faith in God? God knows you need all these things. But if you will only work toward living as God wants you to live, then all these things will be given to you as well."

**Worry Warts: Then maybe we shouldn't worry so much?**

## *Supplies* ..........................................

scissors
pencils
wiggle eyes
craft glue

spray paint designed
for plastic
tapered plastic yogurt
containers

scraps of colored
paper
glue sticks

## Ahead of time:
- Photocopy the directions and patterns for each child.
- Spray paint the yogurt containers with bright colors. Use paint specially designed for plastic.

## Group time:
- Ask: When you go on a trip, what is the first thing you do? Do you pack? Do you wonder about where you will eat or where you will stay? Do you worry about what you will wear? Do you think Jesus has some advice on this?
- Read "Don't Worry!" Let the children be the "worry warts." Teach them the response, which is the same each time except for the last.
- Make a "Don't Worry" Bird.

✂

### "DON'T WORRY" BIRDS

1. Trace and cut the bird parts from colorful paper.
2. Attach the beak to the head as shown.
3. Add wiggle eyes. Set aside to dry.
4. While the head is drying, attach the wings, tail, and Bible verse to the bird as shown.

5. Add the head.
6. Use the bird as a pencil holder to remind you each day not to worry but to trust God.

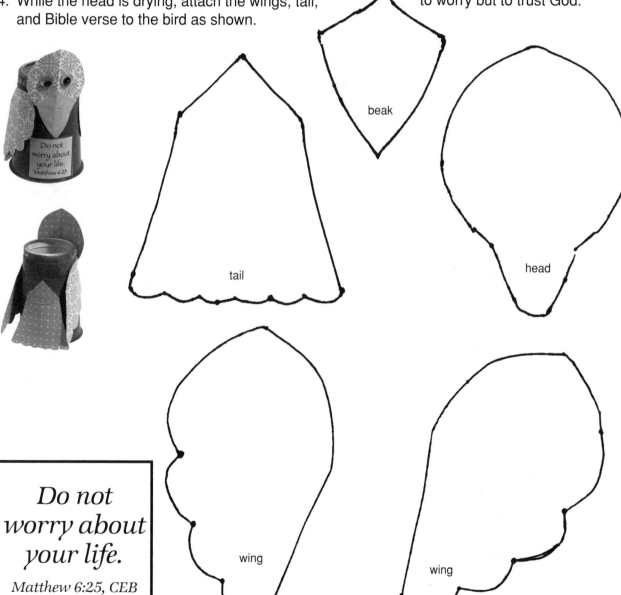

beak

tail

head

*Do not worry about your life.*

Matthew 6:25, CEB

wing

wing

# The Golden Rule

## Bible Story
Matthew 7:12

## Bible Verse
Treat people in the same way that you want people to treat you.

Matthew 7:12, CEB

## Green Message
Jesus teaches us to treat others as we want to be treated.

Everywhere Jesus went, he told the people how God wanted them to live. Sometimes what Jesus taught was so different from what people were used to hearing.

"What's the secret to living as God wants us to?" they asked.

**Jesus said: Do to others as you would have them do to you.**

"What if someone does something bad to me, shouldn't I do something bad back to them? It would teach them a lesson."

**Jesus said: Do to others as you would have them do to you.**

"When someone calls me a bad name or tells lies about me, shouldn't I do the same back to them?" they asked.

**Jesus said: Do to others as you would have them do to you.**

"What if someone takes all my money and even takes my coat? Shouldn't I take their money and coat in return?" they asked.

**Jesus said: Do to others as you would have them do to you.**

"Are you sure this is what God wants?" they asked.

**Jesus said: Do to others as you would have them do to you.**

"If I want people to treat me kindly, do I have to be kind to them first?" they asked.

**Jesus said: Do to others as you would have them do to you.**

"If I want people to be patient with me and help me when I need it, does that mean I have to be patient and helpful first?"

**Jesus said: Do to others as you would have them do to you.**

"If I want people to love one another and share with one another, do I have to show love and share first?"

**Jesus said: It's not hard to love people who love you or to be kind to people who are kind to you. So, do to others as you would have them do to you.**

## Supplies ••••••••••••••••••••••••••••••••••••••

old advertisements or calendars with magnetic backing (see p. 32)

lightweight cardboard (old file folders or cereal boxes)

scissors

crayons or markers

glue sticks

white glue

## Ahead of time:
- Photocopy the directions and bookmark for each child in the group.
- Cut refrigerator magnet ads or calendars into one-inch squares.

## Group time:
- Ask: What are some of the rules you have to follow in your life? Do you like these rules? Did you know that if everyone followed one special rule Jesus gave us, we might not need any other rules?
- Read "The Golden Rule." Have the children say the part in bold type together. (By the end of the session, everyone will know the Golden Rule.)
- Make Golden Rule Bookmarks.

- - - - - - - - - - - - - - - - - - - - - - - - - - - - - - - - - - - - - - - - - - - ✂

### GOLDEN RULER BOOKMARKS

1. Color and cut out the Golden Ruler Bible bookmark.
2. Glue the bookmark onto a piece of lightweight cardboard.
3. Fold on the dotted line.
4. Put glue on the printed side of two magnetic squares. Put the magnets on the back of the bookmark, one on each end.
5. Slip the bookmark over the pages you want to mark. The magnets will hold the bookmark in place.

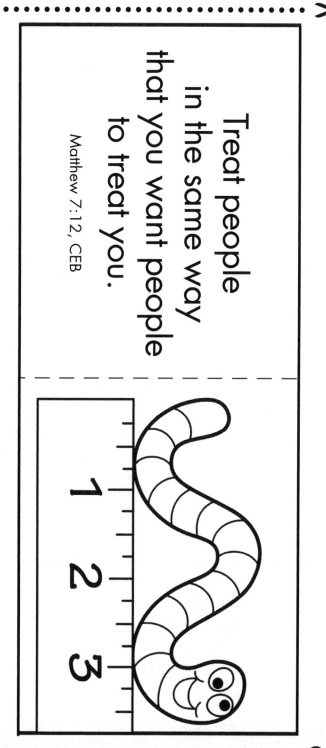

Treat people in the same way that you want people to treat you.

Matthew 7:12, CEB

# Teach Us to Pray

**Bible Story**
Matthew 6:9-13

**Bible Verse**
Lord, teach us to pray.
Luke 11:1, CEB

**Green Message**
We should talk to God every day.

Jesus led a hectic life. Everywhere he went, people followed him. The sick wanted Jesus to heal them.

The crowd shouted, "Heal us, Jesus. Make us well."

The people wanted to understand what Jesus said.

The crowd insisted, "Teach us, Jesus! Teach us."

And everyone wanted Jesus to touch them and bless them.

And the crowd begged, "Bless us, Jesus. Bless us."

So, whenever Jesus found time to go off by himself, it was then that he could talk to God. The disciples saw that Jesus talked to God often. But he did not pray in any of the ways that they understood.

So, the disciples asked him, "Will you teach us to pray?"

This is what Jesus told them, "Do not talk to God as some people do. Their prayers are loud and long. They use many words so that everyone who hears them will be impressed.

Go to a secret place where you can be alone with God. Tell God what is truly in your heart, because God already knows.

And he said the Lord's Prayer to teach them how to talk to God.

*(Guide the children in saying the Lord's Prayer line by line using the following instructions.)*

Praise God. Say that you know that God is holy. *(Read line 1 of the Lord's Prayer. See page 101.)* Talk about your hope that God will come to rule in the hearts of all people everywhere. *(Read line 2.)* Ask God to provide what you truly need. *(Read line 3.)* Ask for God's forgiveness, but be willing to forgive others as well. *(Read line 4.)* Ask for God's help to do the right things and to stay away from that which is truly bad. *(Read Line 5.)* Praise God, the ruler of all Creation. *(Read Lines 6 and 7.)*

## Supplies ......................................................

cardboard
paper punch
scissors
sticks or twigs

string, wire,
   or chenille stems
glue sticks
masking tape

## Ahead of time:

- Cut cardboard into eight- by ten-inch rectangles.
- Photocopy the Lord's Prayer and the hanger directions for each child.
- Cut string, chenille stems, or wire into four-inch lengths.

## Group time:

- Ask: When do you talk to God? What do you say when you talk to God? Where do you talk to God? Did you know that Jesus' friends had never seen anyone talk to God like Jesus did?
- Read "Teach Us to Pray." Assign the lines for the children to read from the prayer.
- Remind the children that prayer should be simple and just like a conversation with God.
- Make the Lord's Prayer Hanger.

---

### THE LORD'S PRAYER HANGER

1. Punch two holes in each corner of a piece of cardboard as shown. Thread a short piece of string or wire through each pair of holes so that the two ends are on the front.
2. Lay the cardboard flat on the table.
3. Cut or break sticks slightly longer than the sides of the cardboard sheet.
4. Lay the sticks on the cardboard as shown, overlapping at the corners.
5. Ask a friend to hold the sticks in place as you secure them with the string or wire.
6. Cut out the Lord's Prayer and glue it in the center of the cardboard frame.
7. Attach a piece of wire to the back with masking tape as a hanger.

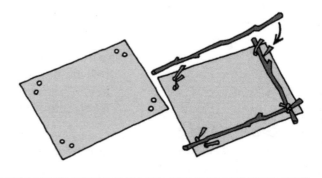

1. Our Father who art in heaven, holy is your name.

2. Thy kingdom come. Thy will be done, on earth as it is in heaven.

3. Give us this day our daily bread.

4. Forgive us our trespasses, as we forgive those who trespass against us.

5. Lead us not into temptation, but deliver us from evil.

6. For thine is the kingdom, and the power, and the glory, forever.

7. Amen.

# Hosanna!

**Bible Story**
Mark 11:1-11

**Bible Verse**
Hosanna! Blessed is the one who comes in the name of the Lord!
Mark 11:9, NRSV

**Green Message**
On Palm Sunday we celebrate Jesus as God's Son.

Spring had come to the land. For all persons of the Jewish faith, it was time to go to Jerusalem to celebrate the Passover. Jesus and his group of friends were on their way.

As they drew near the city, Jesus stopped. "Go into the village. You will find a donkey tied up there. Bring it to me. If anyone tries to stop you, say that 'the Lord needs it and will send it back.'"

The two disciples went into the village and found the donkey tied to a post near the doorway of the house just as Jesus had said. When the owner tried to stop them, the disciples said, "The Lord needs it and will send it back to you."

The two disciples led the donkey back to where Jesus and the others were. They threw their cloaks over the donkey and Jesus climbed on. Then everyone set off down the road to Jerusalem.

When the crowds saw Jesus, they became excited. Some people broke off palm branches and waved them in the air. Some people took off their cloaks and laid them on the road for the donkey to walk on.

Everyone shouted, "Hosanna! Hosanna! Blessed is the one comes in the name of the Lord! Hosanna!"

Persons in the crowd turned to one another and asked, "Who is that person?"

Others answered them, "It is Jesus, the Messiah. The one God sent to save us!"

Soon everyone was shouting, "Hosanna! Hosanna. Blessed is the one comes in the name of the Lord! Hosanna!"

## Supplies ·····························

**recycled newspaper**     **heavy duty scissors**     **masking tape**

## Ahead of time:

- Photocopy the newspaper palm branch directions for each child.
- Separate the newspaper into individual double-sheets. Each child will need two.

## Group time:

- Have the children make the newspaper palm branches.
- Ask: How do we greet important people when they come to town? For example, what would we do if the President came to town?
- Say: Let's see how people in Bible times welcomed someone special.

- Read "Hosanna!" When the time comes to greet Jesus, have the children wave their palm branches.
- If today is Palm Sunday, have a parade of palm branches throughout the church.

### NEWSPAPER PALM BRANCHES

1. Lay one sheet of newspaper out flat.
2. Beginning at the narrow end, tightly roll the newspaper.
3. When the newspaper is two-thirds rolled, insert the second sheet. Continue to roll.
4. When both sheets are rolled into a tube, secure with masking tape around the bottom and about four inches up.
5. From the top end, make four cuts about eight inches long.
6. Reach inside the tube and gently pull the inner layer up.
7. The tube will unroll slightly, the cut areas becoming leaves.

# Remember Me

**Bible Story**
Mark 14:12-16, 22-31

**Bible Verse**
Do this in remembrance of me.
1 Corinthians 11:24, NRSV

**Green Message**
We will remember Jesus and all that he taught.

Jesus and his friends gathered in a room on the roof of a house in Jerusalem. The Passover table was set. Jesus took a seat at the center of the table.

"I have been looking forward to spending Passover with you, my friends," Jesus said. "During this meal we will remember Moses and how with God's help he freed our people. But this will be the last Passover I will celebrate with you."

The disciples looked at one another. "What was Jesus talking about? The last Passover? There would be another Passover next year and the year after and the year after that. Where was Jesus going?" they asked one another.

Jesus held up the special Passover cup. "Here is the cup we drink from at Passover. From now on this cup will have a new meaning. This cup and the wine that is in it will remind you of tonight. Bad things are going to happen. You must be ready."

The disciples looked at one another. "Bad things? What could Jesus be trying to tell them? It didn't sound good."

Then Jesus held up the loaf of bread. "This is the bread that we eat at Passover. This bread will mean something different to you from now on. The authorities are going to arrest me tonight. I will be beaten and put to death. But I do this for you and for others who will come after you."

Jesus held up the cup again. "See this cup! This cup will also remind you that my blood will be spilled and I will die. Every time you drink it, remember me and all that I have taught you."

The disciples looked at Jesus and in their hearts they thought, *We will remember. We will be sad. But we will remember.*

## Supplies ...............................................................

glue sticks
communion elements

scrap paper of different kinds

## Ahead of time:

• Photocopy the tear-a-story directions for each child.

## Group time:

• Display the elements of Communion.
• Ask: Where have you seen these items?
• Say: A long time ago, this bread and this cup were part of another celebration called the Passover. God's people would celebrate this every year to remember how Moses, with God's help, had led the people out of Egypt. Today we remember something else.

• Read "Remember Me."
• Ask: What do we remember during Communion?
• Have the children create a torn paper picture of a favorite Bible story about Jesus. Display them and let the children try to identify each story.

- - - - - - - - - - - - - - - - - - - - - - - - - - - - - - - - - - - - ✂

### A TEAR-A-STORY ABOUT JESUS

1. Choose your favorite story about Jesus.
2. Begin with a plain sheet of paper.
3. Illustrate the story not by drawing, but by tearing paper and gluing it together to make the story picture. No scissors allowed.

4. Have a special show and let your friends try to determine what story you are representing.

# Jesus Asks for Help

**Bible Story**
Mark 14:32-50

**Bible Verse**
The LORD is near to all who call on him.
Psalm 145:18, NRSV

**Green Message**
We can always turn to God in times of trouble.

The Passover meal was over. Most everyone was happily full. But Jesus felt troubled. He needed to talk to God. Jesus invited three of his disciples to come with him to keep watch as he prayed. Jesus knew that the coming trouble would start tonight.

"Keep watch for me," Jesus told them and then he went into the garden. The disciples sat down, leaning against the wall. They closed their eyes—just for a second—and were soon sound asleep.

Jesus knelt down on the ground. He looked up toward heaven. "God, I know why you sent me. I know what you want me to do. I know that you can change this if you want to. But you are wise beyond measure. Whatever you want me to do, I will do."

Jesus got up from the ground and went to where the disciples had been sitting. From inside the garden he could hear their snores. They were sound asleep. "Peter! James! John! Wake up! Can you not stay awake for one short hour?"

The disciples hadn't meant to fall asleep. They had tried to stay awake. But it was so late and they had eaten too much.

Jesus shook his head. "Keep awake! Keep watch! You don't know what's going to happen tonight!" Jesus went back into the garden to pray. "God, you are all powerful. You can stop what is about to happen. Please, I really don't want to do this."

Then once again Jesus got up and went back to the entrance of the garden. Again his friends were asleep. "Is it so hard to stay awake for such a short time? For me?" Jesus went back to pray.

For the third time, Jesus came back to find his friends asleep. But this time it was too late to keep watch. Temple guards with torches were coming up the path to arrest him. The times of trouble had begun. And his disciples...ran away.

But God was with Jesus through it all.

## Supplies..........................................................

| | | |
|---|---|---|
| wax paper | scissors | six-inch paper plates, |
| old crayons | white glue | CDs (circle patterns) |
| plastic knives | iron (adult only) | black construction paper |
| recycled newspaper | battery-operated | lunch-sized paper bags |
| pencils | tea lights | |

## Ahead of time:
- Photocopy the directions and patterns for the prayer luminaria.
- Tear off pieces of wax paper about twelve inches long.

## Group time:
- Ask: What do you do when you are worried about something? Do you ever talk to God about it when you are worried?
- Read "Jesus Asks for Help."
- Ask: What kind of help did Jesus need?

- Ask: Did God make all the bad stuff go away? What did Jesus discover?
- Say: God won't make all the bad stuff go away, but God will be with us through it all.
- Make the prayer luminarias.

✂ - - - - - - - - - - - - - - - - - - - - - - - - - - - - - - - - - - - - - - - - - - - - - - - - - - - - - - ✂

### PRAYER LUMINARIA

1. Use a CD to cut a circle on a paper bag.
2. Fold a piece of wax paper in half. Open.
3. With a plastic knife, shave old and broken crayons over one side of the paper.
4. Close the sheet of wax paper.
5. Place the wax paper sheet between two pieces of newspaper. Press with a warm iron. (The wax crayon will melt.)
6. Place a six-inch paper plate on top of the colored wax paper. Trace. Cut out.

7. Use the pattern to cut praying hands from black construction paper. Glue the hands in the center of the melted wax circle.
8. Add the Bible verse to the front of the bag.
9. Run a bead of glue around the outside edge of the wax paper circle.
10. Slip the circle into the bag and position it over the opening. Press to seal.
11. Place a battery-operated tea light inside the bag.

DO NOT USE A REAL CANDLE.

The LORD is near to all who call on him.
Psalm 145:18, NRSV

# Peter's Rooster

**Bible Story**
Luke 22:54-62

**Bible Verse**
Stand firm in your faith, be brave, be strong.
1 Corinthians 16:13, CEB

**Green Message**
Friends are loyal to one another.

The garden was filled with torches and soldiers and swords. Judas walked right up to Jesus and kissed him on the cheek. The soldiers knew that this was the signal. They were to arrest the man whom Judas kissed. In all the confusion, all the disciples ran away, except for Peter who waited to see what was going on.

The soldiers bound Jesus' hands and led him through the streets to the high priest's house. Peter followed close behind in the shadows so that no one would see him. The soldiers took Jesus inside to meet with the Council. Peter stayed outside in the courtyard.

A servant girl who worked for the high priest brought sticks out to add to the fire. She could tell it was going to be a long night. She spotted Peter standing off to the side. "Hey, you! Don't I know you? You were with that man. I'm sure of it. I saw you with him in the marketplace."

Peter stepped farther back into the shadows. "No, no, you are wrong. I don't know that man. Never saw him before."

Some men in the courtyard drew closer to the fire. One of them looked suspiciously at Peter. "You're one of them. I know I have seen you with that man."

"You are very mistaken," insisted Peter. "I'm not one of THEM."

A second man walked up to Peter. "Wait. Your accent. You are from Galilee. Surely you know that man."

"I don't know what you are talking about. I DO NOT KNOW HIM!" Just then from on top of the courtyard wall, a rooster began to crow.

Peter remembered then what Jesus had said that very night at the Passover meal. "Before the rooster crows in the morning, you will say three times that you don't even know me."

And Peter cried.

## Supplies .......................................................

cardboard tubes
crayons or markers

glue sticks
scissors

## Ahead of time:

- Photocopy the directions for the flapping rooster and the patterns for each child.
- Cut cardboard tubes into three-inch lengths.

## Group time:

- Have the children create their flapping roosters.
- Ask: What does a rooster make you think of? What time of day? Have you ever heard a rooster? How does it sound?
- Say: In today's story the rooster takes on a whole new meaning for one of Jesus' friends.

- Read "Peter's Rooster." Whenever Peter says that he doesn't know Jesus, have the children make their rooster flap its wings.
- Ask: How did Peter feel when he realized he had let his friend down?

### FLAPPING ROOSTER

1. Color and cut out the parts of the rooster.
2. Glue the body wrap to a cardboard tube.
3. Assemble and attach the rooster comb.
4. Fold the wings on the dotted lines. Glue the tabs inside the tube as shown.
5. Cut the pull strip down to the dot. Fold and glue together at the bottom.
6. Thread the pull strip up through the tube from the bottom.
7. Glue tabs A and B to the top of the rooster's wings as shown. Allow time to dry slightly.
8. When the glue is dry, pull down on the pull strip and watch the rooster flap its wings.

# Jesus Is Alive!

**Bible Story**
Matthew 28:1-10

**Bible Verse**
But God raised him
from the dead!
　　　Acts 13:30, CEB

**Green Message**
God is more powerful
than death.

Jesus had been arrested by the soldiers, tried by the Council, and put to death on a cross by the Roman governor. Most of Jesus' friends had gone into hiding, not knowing what to do.

On the day after the sabbath, just as the sun was coming up, Mary Magdalene and the other Mary were on their way to the garden tomb. They came to see the place where Jesus was buried. As they came near the entrance to the garden, the ground began to shake.

It wasn't a real earthquake that caused the ground to shake, but an angel that had come down to earth. The angel went to the tomb and rolled away the stone that had been placed over the entrance. Then the angel sat on the stone.

When the two women came into the garden, that is what they saw. The angel's face was like lightning and its clothing was blindingly white. The two women were so frightened that they almost fell to the ground.

"Don't be afraid," the angel told them. "I know you are looking for Jesus who was crucified. He isn't here. He isn't here because God has raised him from the dead. Come see the place where they laid him."

The women looked inside the tomb and sure enough it was empty. "I have a message for you to give to the disciples," said the angel. "Jesus will meet them in Galilee."

With great fear and excitement the women ran from the garden. On the road back to town they met Jesus himself. They fell to his feet and began to worship him. "Don't be afraid," he said. "Tell the others. I will meet them in Galilee."

Jesus was alive! Jesus was alive and they would see him in Galilee.

## Supplies ........................................................

| | | |
|---|---|---|
| scissors | paper punch | paper (green and blue) |
| cardboard | ribbon or yarn | recycled magazines |
| glue sticks | crayons or markers | |

## Ahead of time:

- Photocopy the cross and directions for each child.
- Cut cardboard into eight- by ten-inch rectangles.

## Group time:

- Ask: Why do we celebrate Easter? What special thing happened on that Easter morning? Has that ever happened before? Since?
- Read "Jesus Is Alive!"
- Say: God is more powerful than death.

- Say: Just as Jesus said he would, God raised Jesus from the dead. Jesus is alive and with us today.
- Have the children make mosaic crosses to celebrate that God raised Jesus from the dead.

### MOSAIC CROSS

1. Cut out the cross below.
2. Cut about 26–30 thumb-sized pieces from colorful pages in old magazines.
3. Glue the pieces onto the cross, covering the entire surface but letting the black show through around each piece.
4. Trim edges that extend beyond the cross.
5. Cover a piece of cardboard with blue paper for sky and green paper for ground.

6. Punch holes at the top about one inch from each side.
7. Glue the cross onto the cardboard.
8. Thread ribbon through the two holes at the top and tie in a bow.
9. Write "Jesus lives!" on the poster.

# On the Emmaus Road

**Bible Story**
Luke 24:13-35

**Bible Verse**
The Lord really has risen!
   Luke 24:34, CEB

**Green Message**
Jesus is alive and in the world with us today.

**Pronunciation:**
Cleopas (KLEE oh-puhs)

Cleopas and Simon had run all the way back from Emmaus. Then they ran to find the place where the disciples were staying. "You ...will...never... guess...who ...we...just...had ....dinner...with!" said Cleopas, panting.

"What could be so important that you had to run all the way back to the city? You ran seven miles, at night, in the dark? What could possibly be so important?" asked Peter.

"We saw Jesus. He joined us on the road. But at first we didn't know who he was. We invited him to stay the evening with us and share the meal. That's when we knew," said Simon.

"What did you know?" asked Peter.

"We knew that he was Jesus. When he took the bread, blessed it, and then gave it to us. We knew," said Simon.

"That's right! Then when he took the bread, blessed it and broke it, we knew it was Jesus. We should have known earlier as we traveled the road," said Cleopas.

"He told us things about himself that only he would know," said Simon. "Our hearts burned within us. We should've known!"

"Yes," said Cleopas. "We should have known!"

"What happened after dinner?" asked James.

"He left," said Simon.

"Left to go where?" asked John.

"We don't know. One minute he was there, the next minute he was gone. That's when we knew we had to come back here and tell you. Jesus is alive! The stories ARE true."

## Supplies .............................................

scissors
glue sticks
recycled magazines

paper fasteners
crayons or markers
sheet of paper

## Ahead of time:

- Photocopy the directions and the bread pattern for each child.
- Seal the envelopes and fold them in half. Cut along the fold. (One envelope will make two baskets.)
- To save time, use a paper cutter to cut one- by eight inch strips from magazine pages.
- Cut out a picture from a magazine and glue it onto a piece of paper.

## Group time:

- Hold up the picture where the children can't see it and begin to describe it (accurately or not). Ask the children if they think you are being truthful. Then ask another child to confirm your description.
- Ask: Is it easier to believe something is true if someone else confirms it? Why?

- Say: After the women told the story of Jesus' Resurrection, some people didn't believe them. It took other people confirming it to make it real.
- Read "On the Emmaus Road."
- Ask: What was it that Jesus did that convinced the men that he was Jesus?
- Make the bread and basket.

### THE BREAD AND BASKET

1. Hold half of a nine- by twelve-inch envelope so that the open end is up.
2. Cut eight evenly spaced slits from the bottom. Stop about an inch from the top.
3. Weave colorful strips from magazine pages in and out of the slits on one side. Secure the ends with glue.
4. Turn the envelope over and weave the strips on the second side. Glue the ends.
5. Color and cut out the "bread."
6. Attach the two pieces of bread and Bible verse with a paper fastener. (The Bible verse is behind the two pieces of bread.)
7. Put the bread into the basket.

# With Us Always

**Bible Story**
Matthew 28:16-20

**Bible Verse**
And remember, I am with you always.
Matthew 28:20,
NRSV

**Green Message**
Jesus will be with us now and forever.

My name is John. One day Jesus came by and said to my brother and me, "Follow me." And we did. Our lives changed from that day on. I was one of Jesus' first disciples. James and Peter and I were part of the inner circle of disciples. But we learned that even though we were part of the "in group," we were no more important in God's kingdom than anyone else.

Today, along with ten other disciples, I am on the way to Galilee, to the hillside where we often met when Jesus was alive. It's a long trip from Jerusalem to Galilee. But when Mary discovered the empty tomb and actually saw Jesus, he told her to tell the rest of us to go to Galilee. That is where we would find him. If that is where Jesus is going to be, then that is where we are going!

I believe in my heart that Jesus has something special for us to do. I wonder what it is. But whatever it is, he wants to tell us in person.

When we get to the hillside, we see Jesus. He is sitting in the usual place. We all begin to run to him and fall at his feet, worshiping him.

"Friends," he says to us, "All authority in heaven and on earth has been given to me. What I want you to do is to go to all nations. Make new disciples. Teach them to obey everything that I have commanded you. And remember this: I will be with you always."

We turned to one another. This would not be easy job. "All nations?" we asked one another. This would mean telling people who are different from us. Are they allowed to be Christians too?

Once again our lives will change. But the one thing we can count on is that Jesus will be with us always—no matter where we go or what we do. And always is a very long time.

## Supplies

plastic lids
white glue
cotton swabs

paper punch
art tissue (greens,
blues, browns)

yarn or ribbon

## Ahead of time:
- Photocopy the directions and earth guides for each child.
- Pour white glue into shallow containers, one for each child.

## Group time:
- Ask: What happened on Easter Sunday? What did Jesus tell the women to tell the other disciples?
- Read "With Us Always."
- Say: Going to all nations to tell others about Jesus was going to be hard for the disciples. They had always stuck to people just like themselves. But Jesus changed all that.
- Make the "All the Earth" hangers.

TIP: *See the front cover of this book for a photograph of this craft.*

- - - - - - - - - - - - - - - - - - - - - - - - - - - - - - - - - - - - - - - - - ✂

### "ALL THE EARTH" HANGERS

1. Cut out the earth circle below.
2. Glue it to the center of a plastic lid.
3. Pour white glue into shallow containers (such as other plastic lids).
4. Cut or tear colored art tissue into pieces about one inch square.
5. Wad up each piece of art tissue, dip it lightly in the white glue and press it onto the design—blues for the ocean, greens and browns for the land.
6. When the design is completely covered, if there is still space on the lid, create a "frame" around the picture.
7. Allow to dry slightly. Then turn the lid over and glue the Bible verse on the back.
8. Punch a hole at the top edge and tie a ribbon.

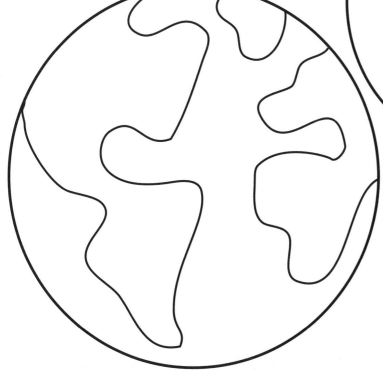

# Dancing for Joy

**Bible Story**
Acts 3:1-10

**Bible Verse**
He entered the temple with them, walking, leaping, and praising God.

Acts 3:8b, CEB

**Green Message**
We can spread the good news about Jesus by what we say and do.

Peter and John were two of Jesus' disciples. They had been to the mountain. They had seen their friend and teacher after his Resurrection. They had a new job to do.

One day the two men were going up to the Temple to pray. A man who had been lame from birth called out to them.

"Please help me!" he cried. "I cannot work! I cannot earn a living! Please give me what you can!"

Peter stopped and looked at the man. "I don't have any money. But I do have something to give you. In the name of Jesus the Christ, get up and walk!"

At first the man was confused and just looked at Peter. He couldn't believe what Peter had said. But then the man began to feel strength flow into his legs. He carefully stood up. He walked. Then he was dancing and leaping for joy.

The man shouted as he danced, "Praise God! Praise God! You have given me the greatest gift of all. Praise God."

People who were standing nearby could not believe what they were seeing. They had never seen anything like it. All Peter had done was hold the man's hand and tell him to get up and walk. But not only was the man walking, but he was leaping and dancing. Who were these men? By what power did they do such a wonderful thing?

"We do this not of our own power," said Peter, "but through the power of Jesus Christ. This is the one YOU put to death and who was raised by God. The name of Jesus has made this man strong."

Soon the word of what Peter and John were able to do spread around the town.

## Supplies • • • • • • • • • • • • • • • • • • • • • • • • • • • • • •

**long, narrow snack cake boxes**
**elastic or rubber bands**
**scissors**

**crayons or markers**
**craft glue**
**paper punch**

## Ahead of time:
- Photocopy the "happy feet" directions and cut-outs.
- Cut long snack cake boxes in half and make half-moon cuts as shown so that they will fit snugly against the ankle.

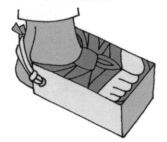

## Group time:
- Ask: After Jesus' resurrection, what do you think the disciples did? Do you think they wanted to share the news with everyone?
- Read "Dancing for Joy."
- Ask: How did Peter and John share the good news of Jesus with the man at the Temple? How did the man respond?
- Have the children make "Happy Feet" and do a happy dance to celebrate the good news.

### HAPPY FEET

1. Color and cut out the "happy feet" and glue to the top of the boxes.
2. Punch a hole in the short sides of each box near the open end.
3. Tightly tie each end of a piece of elastic or rubber band through the holes.
4. Remove your shoes and slide your feet into the boxes.
5. Pull the elastic around your heel and dance!

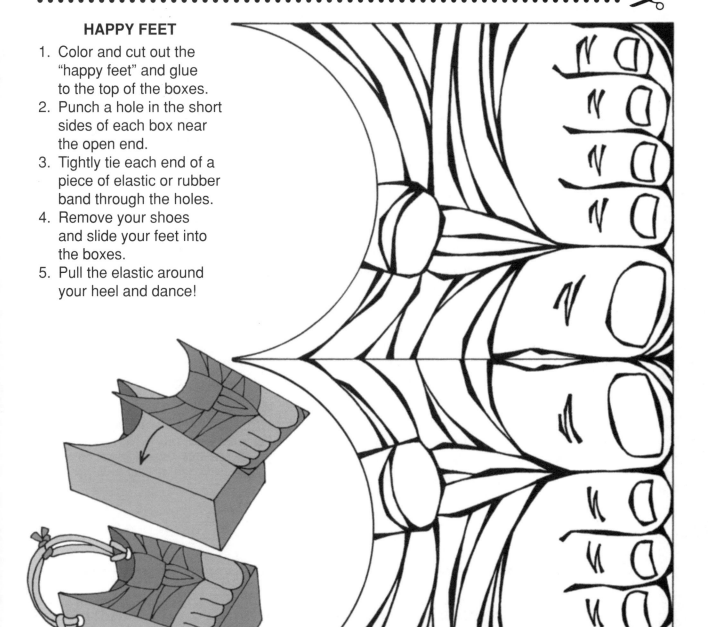

# Hearts of Fire

**Bible Story**
Acts 2:1-21

**Bible Verse**
I will pour out my
Spirit on all people.
Acts 2:17, CEB

**Green Message**
God empowers us to
spread the good news
to all people.

Before Jesus was arrested, before he was put to death, before God raised him from the dead, Jesus made a promise to his friends. "I am going to leave you. But after I leave, God will send you a helper."

And his friends wondered, *What will this helper be like?*

"This helper will fill your heart with fire!" Jesus said. "You will tell the world about me. In fact, you won't be able to keep it all inside. It will come pouring out—to everyone you meet."

And his friends wondered, *How will this helper help?*

"This helper will be a companion and a comfort to you," said Jesus. "With this helper, you will never be alone. This helper will always be with you—on the darkest night, the longest road, the loneliest place. When you are sad, this helper will be there to cheer you up.

And his friends wondered, *What else will this helper do?*

"This helper will give you power and boldness," said Jesus. "The power to do what is right. The power to make good choices and live as I have taught you. You will need to be bold in order to spread my message to all the world."

Then one day, when the disciples were gathered in a room together, the Holy Spirit came to them. It came as a rush of wind. *(Have the children make the sound of the wind.)* Flames hovered over the heads of the disciples. *(Wave the fire wands overhead.)* And everyone began to speak—not in just their own language, but all the languages of the world. *(Have the children each begin to sing a song that they like.)*

The disciples felt fire in their hearts. They felt comforted. They felt power and boldness. The disciples were ready to spread the good news everywhere. The church was on the move. *(Have the children get up and march around the room with their wands.)*

## Supplies ...............................................................

recycled newspaper
stapler, staples

heavy-duty scissors
tape (red and clear)

red and white
plastic bags

## Ahead of time:

- Photocopy the fire wand directions for each child.
- Separate newspaper into single sheets.

## Group time:

- Ask: When is your birthday? What do you do on your birthday? Did you know that the church has a birthday day too?
- Make the fire wands.
- Read "Hearts of Fire." Have the children provide the sound effects and the visuals with the fire wands.

- Ask: What gave the disciples the power to spread the good news about Jesus?
- Say: The Holy Spirit is alive and well in the world today. It gives us power and boldness. It sets our hearts afire. It gives us comfort. Like the disciples, we can spread the good news about Jesus to everyone.

- - - - - - - - - - - - - - - - - - - - - - - - - - - - - - - - - - - - ✂

## FIRE WANDS

1. Stack two or three red and white plastic bags in a neat, flat pile.
2. Staple several times along the bottom edge, positioning the staples so that they run parallel to the sides of the bags.
3. Trim off the handle sections and the bottom folds as shown.
4. Cut ¾-inch-wide strips into the unstapled end of the bags. Stop your cuts about an inch or so from the stapled edge.

5. Fold a single sheet of newspaper in half (top to bottom), in half (side to side), and then in half (side to side) again.
6. Roll into a tube and tape at the top and bottom. This will be the handle.
7. Wrap the stapled end of the bags around one end of the handle.
8. Wrap the handle with red tape, including the stapled ends of the plastic bags.

# C-H-R-I-S-T-I-A-N

**Bible Story**
Acts 11:19-26

**Bible Verse**
It was in Antioch that the disciples were first called "Christians."
Acts 11:26c, NRSV

**Green Message**
Those people who follow Jesus and live as Jesus taught are called "Christians."

For believers in Jerusalem,
Life wasn't very fun.
They could not meet or worship,
They were always on the run.

*(whisper)* I am a C-H-R-I-S-T-I-A-N!    CHRISTIAN!

So some of them packed up their things
And headed out of town,
For if they planned to live at all,
They should not hang around.

*(whisper)* I am a C-H-R-I-S-T-I-A-N!    CHRISTIAN!

They fled to cities near and far,
But the good news went along.
At first their numbers were quite small,
But their faith was very strong.

*(a little louder)* I am a C-H-R-I-S-T-I-A-N!    CHRISTIAN!

In spite of all the new church grew.
There seemed no end in sight.
And when the Gentiles heard the word,
They knew they'd seen the light.

*(a little louder)* I am a C-H-R-I-S-T-I-A-N!    CHRISTIAN!

It was in a place called Antioch
Where good news was proclaimed,
That all who worshiped Jesus Christ
At last received their name.

*(shout)* I am a C-H-R-I-S-T-I-A-N!    CHRISTIAN!

## Supplies ·············································

cardboard tubes
paper punch
scissors
glue sticks
masking tape

large wooden beads
(10 per child)
crayons or markers
art supplies for
decorating

paper cutter
(optional)
yarn or string

## Ahead of time:
- With a paper cutter, cut cardboard tubes into two-inch sections.

## Group time:
- Ask: Do you ever wonder how so many people all over the world came to know about Jesus?
- Say: At first the followers of Jesus were just tolerated. Then they were hated. They had to leave town in a hurry.
- Read "C–H–R–I–S–T–I–A–N."
- Make a C–H–R–I–S–T–I–A–N mobile.

---

### C–H–R–I–S–T–I–A–N MOBILES

1. Cut apart the letters. Glue each to a two-inch cardboard tube as shown.
2. Punch two holes in each tube as shown.
3. Decorate the tubes and letters with crayons and markers or other art supplies.
4. Beginning with a wooden bead, string the letters onto the string or yarn, starting with the last letter in the word *Christian*.
5. Tie a loop at the top for hanging.

HINT: *Wrap the end of the string or yarn with masking tape to make it easier to thread the beads and letter pieces.*

punch holes

# A Daring Escape!

## Bible Story
Acts 9:1-25

## Bible Verse
We are God's servants, working together.
1 Corinthians 3:9, NRSV

## Green Message
Christians work together to help one another.

Before Paul became a follower of Jesus, he tried to put Christians in prison. He would hear rumors about Christians in a city and he would go there. One day on his way to arrest Christians who lived in Damascus, Jesus appeared to Paul in a vision. It was scary, because for three days Paul could not see. When his sight was returned, Paul was a different person. So he decided to stay in the city and tell how Jesus, the Son of God, had changed his life.

"Isn't this the man who used to arrest Christians? What changed him?" the people would ask.

"Can we trust him?" other people said. "What if he changes back and tries to arrest us?"

But Paul stayed in Damascus for a long time, preaching and teaching. The group of Christians grew and grew. Then one day some of the Jewish leaders in the city decided that it was time to get rid of Paul and put an end to his preaching.

"Paul is growing powerful. Too many people are listening to him. Soon they won't listen to us," said one of the leaders. "We'd better stop him before everyone becomes a follower of Jesus."

The leaders got together and came up with a plan to get rid of Paul permanently. Some of Paul's new friends heard about the plan and decided to help. "We need to get him out of the city in order to save his life. But first we must get him past the guards at the city gate."

"Let's lower him down the wall one night," one friend suggested. Late one night Paul and his friends went to a house that was built into the wall around the city. They lowered Paul down the wall in a large basket. Then Paul quickly left the area. The Jewish leaders never did discover how Paul got out of the city. And Paul continued to tell the story of Jesus, the Son of God.

## Supplies ●●●●●●●●●●●●●●●●●●●●●●●●●●●●●●●●●●●●●●●●●●

scrap paper
crayons or markers

colored duct tape
scissors

## Ahead of time:

- Photocopy the coupon holder directions for each child.
- Cut scrap paper into five- by four-inch rectangles.

## Group time:

- Say: Everyone likes to help. In today's story a man's life was saved because his friends came up with a daring plan. Let's see what happened.
- Read "A Daring Escape!"
- Ask: Why did the leaders want to get rid of Paul? How did his friends help him escape?

TIP: *You may wish to cut the nine-inch strips of colored duct tape in advance to save time. Do this shortly before the session begins and be careful to keep the strips separate.*

- Say: We may not be able to save someone's life, but we can find ways to help that will make a difference.
- Make the coupon holder and some coupons to go inside.

✂

## DUCT TAPE COUPON HOLDER

1. Place a nine-inch strip of duct tape sticky side up on the table.
2. Place another strip so that the top edge overlaps the bottom edge of the first strip.
3. Add two more strips in the same way.
4. Now place a strip sticky side down on each of the first four strips.
5. Trim the edges so they are even.
6. Fold the rectangle as shown here, so that one side is slightly taller than the other.
7. Seal the edges with two smaller pieces of duct tape. Use a different color.
8. Create coupons of things you can do in the coming week that will help others. Place them in the holder.

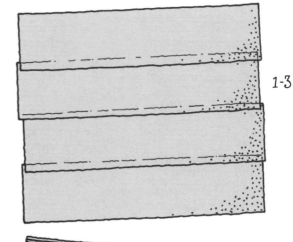

1-3

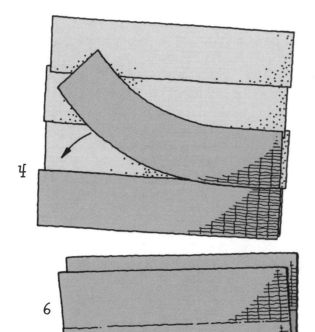

4

6

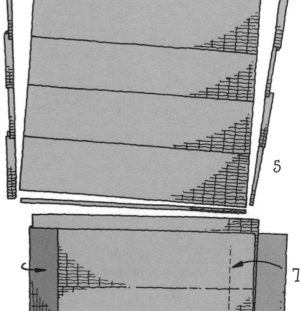

5

7

# I Believe!

**Bible Story**
Acts 16:16-40

**Bible Verse**
I by my works will show you my faith.
James 2:18, NRSV

**Green Message**
We show others that we are disciples of Jesus by what we say and do.

Refrain:

Paul and Silas, Silas and Paul
Told about Jesus to one and to all.

One day our friends were walking down the streets of Philippi,
When a servant girl accused them of serving God Most High.
She shouted it quite loudly 'till the two men turned about,
And in the name of Jesus Christ, Paul cast her demons out.

Refrain

The owners of this servant girl did not think this was funny
Because they needed all her skills to earn them lots of money.
Soon Paul and Silas found themselves inside a prison's walls,
Where they were soundly beaten for breaking several laws.

Refrain

But even though these two men were shackled to the wall,
Their prayers to God and songs of praise inspired one and all.
That night an earthquake shook the jail; it cracked the prison floors.
It broke their chains and set them free. It opened all the doors.

Refrain

Now when the jailer heard the noise, he knew what he would see,
With no locks on the prison doors, the inmates would be free.
But when the jailer looked inside, how shocked he was to see,
That every single prisoner was right where he should be!

Refrain

The jailer knelt upon the floor at Paul's unshackled feet.
"I know that you are men of God, salvation I now seek."
"It isn't hard," the two men said, "God's pardon you'll receive.
And all you have to do is say, 'Lord Jesus, I believe.'"

## Supplies

| | | |
|---|---|---|
| key | clear tape or glue | masking or duct tape |
| scissors | 15-ounce soup cans | |
| crayons or markers | black yarn | |

124

## Ahead of time:
- Photocopy the "Keys to the Kingdom" cut-outs and directions.
- Cut black yarn into twelve-inch pieces, eight per child.

## Group time:
- Hold up an old key. Ask: What do you think this will open? Did you know that we have a key that will open the kingdom of heaven?
- Say: In case you don't remember, Paul was a special missionary whom Jesus chose to tell others the good news about him. Silas was his friend.
- Read "I Believe!" Have the children say the refrain.
- Ask: Why were Paul and Silas in prison? Did they act like most prisoners? What did they do? What happened to them? Did the prisoners all run away? What did Paul and Silas tell the jailer? What is the key to the kingdom of heaven?
- Make "Keys to the Kingdom."

✂

### KEYS TO THE KINGDOM

1. Color and cut out the can wrap and the Bible verse key.
2. Tape or glue the Paul and Silas wrap on the front of the soup can.
3. Tape or glue the Bible verse key on the back of the can.
4. Lay the pieces of yarn across the bottom of the soup can as shown. Tape securely with masking tape or duct tape.
5. Bring the ends of the yarn up to the top edge of the can and tape individually on the inside using masking tape or duct tape.

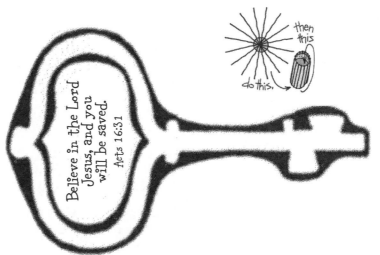

Believe in the Lord Jesus, and you will be saved. Acts 16:31

# Get Up and Go!

**Bible Story**
Acts 8:26-40

**Bible Verse**
I am eager to learn all that you want me to do; help me to understand more and more.
Psalm 119:32, CEV

**Green Message:**
God wants us to spread the good news of Jesus everywhere we go.

**Pronunciation:**
Gaza (GAY-zuh)

Before Jesus left to be with God, he told his disciples that they must go to all nations and spread the good news. But Jesus didn't tell them how. Philip waited for direction.

One day an angel appeared to Philip. "Get up, Philip. Get up now. You've got a job to do. Go down to the Gaza Road. There you will find someone who needs you."

Philip went to the place that the angel had told him about. He saw a government official riding in a chariot. He wondered to himself, *Maybe this is the person who needs my help. I think I will run alongside the chariot and wait for guidance.*

The man in the chariot was reading out loud from the Book of Isaiah. "These words are confusing," he said. "I don't know what they mean. I need someone to help me."

Philip knew then that he was in the right place. Here was something he could do. "Excuse me, sir, may I help you?"

The official stopped the chariot. "I am so confused. The prophet Isaiah is talking about someone that God will send. How will I know who it is?"

Philip climbed up into the chariot beside the man. "I know who it is. I will tell you about him. His name is Jesus." Philip told the man all about Jesus. He told him about his teachings. Most importantly, he told the man how God had raised Jesus from the dead.

"You are a gift from God!," said the official. "You know the answers to all my questions. I want to be a follower of Jesus. Can you baptize me?"

"Jesus told us to baptize people in the name of God the Father, in the name of Jesus the Son, and in the name of the Holy Spirit. So that I can do." Philip baptized the official. Now there was one more follower of Jesus to spread the word.

## Supplies ••••••••••••••••••••••••••••••••••••••••

- 8-ounce milk or juice cartons
- utility knife (adult only)
- heavy duty scissors
- colored paper
- white glue
- 10 ¾-ounce soup cans
- old file folders
- paper punch
- paper fasteners
- crayons or markers
- optional: spray paint for plastic (gold, silver, or bright color)
- yarn

## Ahead of time:

- Photocopy the chariot directions for each child.
- Cut away the top part of the milk cartons with a utility knife. (Adult only.)
- COOL OPTION: *Spray paint the cartons in gold, silver, or a bright color.*

## Group time:

- Make up a sentence in jibberish. Say it to the children again and again.
- Say: I'll say it in English. Today's story is about someone who "translated" the Bible message about Jesus for a person who didn't understand.
- Read "Get Up and Go!"
- Ask: How did Philip make a new disciple for Jesus Christ? How can we tell others about Jesus, too?
- Make the Ethiopian's chariot.

- - - - - - - - - - - - - - - - - - - - - - - - - - - - - - - - - - - - - - - - - - - - ✂

### THE ETHIOPIAN'S CHARIOT

1. Cut the sides and back of a milk carton to make a chariot. Cover with colored paper. (COOL OPTION: *Use spray paint instead.*)
2. Use a small soup can as a pattern to cut two wheels from an old file folder. Decorate.
3. Poke a hole on each side of the chariot.
4. Attach the wheels using paper fasteners.
5. Color and cut out the Ethiopian and his horse. Glue each to an old file folder. Trim. Fold where the arrows show.
6. Punch holes on the horse and chariot as shown and add yarn for reins.

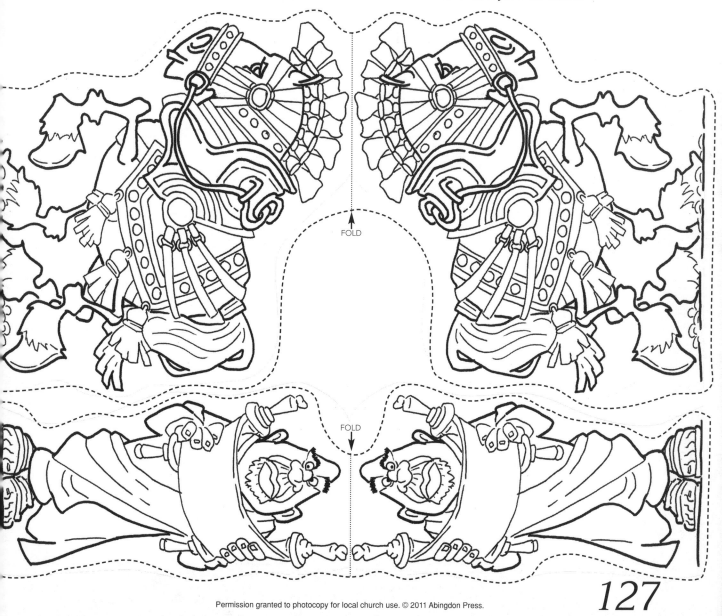

FOLD

FOLD

127

# Scripture Index

## Old Testament

## New Testament

*This book is dedicated to my Aunt Spence, my "other mother," who taught me how to make something wonderful out of anything.*